REDEMPTION
Accomplished
and
Applied

REDEMPTION ACCOMPLISHED AND APPLIED—CTC 304
by
Donald N. Bowdle, Ph.D., Th.D.

REDEMPTION
Accomplished
and
Applied

DONALD N. BOWDLE

PATHWAY PRESS · CLEVELAND, TENNESSEE

To my grandfather,
ROBERT ELMER BOWDLE
(1881-   )
and to the memory of my grandmother,
EFFIE LEGATES BOWDLE
(1882-1940),
firstfruits of the Church of God
on Maryland's Eastern Shore,
I dedicate this volume.

THE CHURCH TRAINING COURSE SERIES

REDEMPTION ACCOMPLISHED AND AP-
PLIED is written by Donald N. Bowdle, Ph.D.,
Th.D. and is one of the study books in the special
study course (CTC 304). A "Certificate of Credit"
is awarded on the basis of the following requirements:

I. The written review and instructions for pre-
paring the review are listed on pages 119, 120.
The written review must be completed, re-
viewed by the pastor or someone whom he may
designate, and the name of the student sent to
the state office. (No grade will be given for
the written review.)

II. The book must be read through.

III. Training sessions must be attended unless per-
mission for absence is granted by the instructor.

IV. The written review is not an examination, but
is designated to review the text and reinforce
the information presented in the text. Students
should research the text for the proper answers.

V. Church Training Course credit may be secured
by home study, if no classes are conducted in
this course of study.

A training record should be kept in the local
church for each person who studies this and other
courses in the Church Training Course program. A
record form, CTC 33, will be furnished upon re-
quest from the state office.

FOREWORD

My first acquaintance with Donald N. Bowdle came when I became a member of the Unity Sunday School Class at the North Cleveland Church of God where he was ministering as teacher. I looked forward to every opportunity of attending that class because he possessed a most remarkable ability to make the truths of the Bible so real and meaningful. He could take the most complex scripture, or passage of scripture, and make it so simple that even I could understand it clearly. This is one of the identifying marks of a truly great teacher. Since those days of our first acquaintance, I have come to admire and appreciate Don Bowdle for the many ways in which he has allowed God to use him.

In addition to being an outstanding teacher, he is a prolific writer, an excellent speaker, a gifted theologian, as well as an anointed preacher. He is a product of the Church of God, a native of Easton, Maryland, and an ordained minister in the Church of God. Don lives in Cleveland, Tennessee with his wife, Nancy, and their two children, Keven and Karen, where they are members of Westmore Church. He is currently serving as Professor of History and Religion, and Chairman of the Department of History, at Lee College.

Don's preparation for his illustrious ministry has been extensive. He earned the B.A. degree *magna cum laude* in religion and history from Lee College and graduate degrees of M.A. and Ph.D. in New Testament language and literature from Bob Jones University, Th.M. in ancient and medieval church history from Princeton Theological Seminary, and Th.D. in American church history from Union Theological Seminary in Virginia.

At Princeton he was awarded a Samuel Robinson Foundation Scholarship, and at Union the Robert C. and Sadie G. Anderson Foundation Scholarship for Graduate Study. Don has taught European and American history at Virginia Commonwealth University in Richmond, and continues as book reviewer for the influential *Richmond Times-Dispatch,* with nearly one hundred published reviews to date, and as regular contributor to the quarterly *Religious and Theological Abstracts.* His most recent work has been the editing of *Ellicott's Bible Commentary* (Zondervan, 1971).

At Lee his peers have elected him to *Who's Who in American Education, Outstanding Educators of America, Outstanding Young Men of America,* and *Personalities of the South.* Listed in *International Scholars Directory* and *Dictionary of International Biography,* he is an active member of the Southern Historical Association, the American Society of Church History, the Society of Biblical Literature, the Evangelical Theological Society, the Society for Pentecostal Studies, and the Academy of Christians in the Professions.

The author was commissioned by the General Board of Youth and Christian Education to prepare a study text on the subject, "God's Plan of Redemption." He has chosen to title his work *Redemption Accomplished and Applied.* I have read and reread the manuscript several times and should like to commend the author for his excellent treatment of the subject. I have been tremendously blessed and enlightened in biblical truth by having studied the manuscript. I would suggest that the person who studies this Church Training Course select, as I did, two valuable books to assist him: a copy of the Holy Bible and a good dictionary. The biblical truths set forth in this book are well documented, and the student should read each scripture as it is noted in the text. Also, the author uses many terms that are not familiar to the average reader. Instead of skipping over these terms, the student should look them up so that he may get the full meaning of the message. After all, if a study course does not challenge our thinking and enlarge our understanding, it is much less than a good study course. It is my belief that anyone who takes time to thoroughly study and consider the plan of redemption as explained by Dr. Bowdle will certainly have a clearer understanding of God's greatest expression of His love for mankind.

In keeping with the policy concerning Church Training Course books of a doctrinal nature, this text was submitted to and approved by the General Executive Council of the Church of God.

Paul F. Henson,
General Director of
Youth and Christian Education

Dear dying Lamb, Thy precious blood
   Shall never lose its pow'r,
Till all the ransomed Church of God
   Be saved, to sin no more.
          —William Cowper

PREFACE

Nearly twenty years have passed since I entered the ministry during the tenures of the Reverend W. C. Byrd, Overseer of Maryland, and the Reverend William F. Morris, pastor at Easton. This present volume, together with my recent edition of *Ellicott's Bible Commentary* (Zondervan, 1971), represents a continuing ambition to render some permanent contribution to God and His Church beyond pulpit and lecture hall. I trust that it will be received with the same eagerness and charity as that with which it is offered.

This book is predicated upon the conviction that an intellectually responsible and thoroughly relevant Pentecostalism is our most urgent need. Peter has insisted upon being "ready always to give an answer to every man that asketh you a reason of the hope that is in you with meekness and fear" (1 Peter 3:15). This is not an option but an imperative.

To that end, therefore, this volume has been designed as a study manual, requiring more than a cursory reading. Throughout the whole I have introduced numerous theological terms—always with definition—which represent important biblical concepts, and of which each of us must have some elemental understanding if he is to communicate this "good news" with clarity and power. I have offered, as well, a minimum of Greek and Hebrew helps for those with facility in the languages of Holy Scripture; otherwise, the explanations are sufficient in themselves.

Preparation of a volume of this nature has been a spiritual as well as an academic experience. I have been impressed again with the magnitude of God's redemptive plan, and praise Him that "whosoever

will"—even I!—should be included in it. And I
have become committed afresh to a positive posture
respecting the providence of God in human history,
which, as I remember hearing Dr. Albert Outler say,
is to the Christian more than "a cosmic analogy of
Linus' blanket." It is that singular truth upon which
we must learn to lean most heavily, because it alone
offers a pattern to the puzzle of life. (See Romans 8:
28-39.)

The reader is reminded that exigencies of space
necessarily precluded both detailed discussions of
doctrine and lengthy citation of biblical passages. I
have, however, attempted to give copious documen-
tation in terms of references; the reader, therefore,
would do well to study this book with Bible in hand.
Unless otherwise indicated, the passages quoted follow the Authorized (King James) Version.

I am indebted for my title to Dr. John Murray's
Redemption Accomplished and Applied (Eerdmans, 1955), which conveys so well the scope and
intent of my work here. For their continuing concern for my ministry, I acknowledge my parents, Mr.
and Mrs. Nelson E. Bowdle; for her constant encour-
agement and substantial help in this project, as in
all other of my undertakings, I thank my wife,
Nancy, helpmate extraordinary; for their challenge
and blessing to my life, I recognize my children,
Keven and Karen; and for their persistent spirit of
inquiry, I express appreciation to my colleagues and
students at Lee College.

Donald N. Bowdle

CONTENTS

PART ONE

REDEMPTION ACCOMPLISHED

That God's plan is of eternal design is a most marvelous and essential tenet of His Word. The entire revelation of salvation history is a circle, with creation, redemption, and consummation being those paramount *loci* or focal points on the perimeter. Jesus Christ is the King of salvation history, occupying the center of that revelatory circle and illuminating the whole. Thus Paul exclaimed: "Now unto the King of the ages, the incorruptible, invisible God, be honour and glory *from eternity to eternity*. Amen" (1 Timothy 1:17).[1]

As a record of salvation history, the Bible is one coherent whole. It is more than mere words in ink on paper; it is an organism throbbing with life, certifying that the redemptive will of God has been effected in history according to an eternal plan, graduated or progressive in its disclosure, magnifying Christ as Lord throughout.

Part One of this study concerns man's need of redemption and God's gracious provision of it in His Son.

---

1 So rendered by Erich Sauer, *The Dawn of World Redemption; A Survey of Historical Revelation in the Old Testament*, trans. G. H. Lang (Grand Rapids, Michigan: Wm. B. Eerdmans Publishing Company, 1955), p. 13. Cf. 1 Corinthians 15:28: ". . . that God may be all in all."

1

The Creation and Original Condition of Man

Anthropology is the doctrine of man. The term has scientific, philosophical, and theological usages, depending upon the aspect of man being investigated. Scientific anthropology treats man in his psycho-physical organism and natural history; philosophical anthropology enlarges its concern to his psychology, sociology, and ethics, together with his anatomy and physiology; theological anthropology deals with his relation to God. Man is, indeed, a complex creature, with material, societal, and spiritual dimensions to his being.

The Greek word for "man" is *anthropos*. This generic term is usually considered an Attic composite, being derived from *ano* ("up"), *athrein* ("to look"), and *eis opa* ("into the face").[1] Thus man is one who "looks up into the face of"; *i.e.*, erect, and unlike the quadrupeds with downward gaze, man looks up into the face of his Creator, intimating by this posture rational and moral capacities.

---

1 See Henry George Liddell and Robert Scott, *A Greek-English Lexicon* (ninth edition; Oxford: Oxford University Press, 1940), pp. 33, 141-2, 2042.

NATURALISM AND SUPERNATURALISM

As in the case of the origin of the universe in general, so in the matter of the beginnings of man in particular, naturalism and supernaturalism constitute two clearly defined camps. With regard to the former problem, *rapprochement* or reconciliation between naturalism and supernaturalism apparently has been achieved; but respecting the latter issue, as far as our present level of understanding is concerned, polarization of camps clearly is the stance.

On the Origin of the Earth

Natural science presently supposes that planets and stellar bodies were formed in the primeval past by the explosion of a so-called "cosmic egg." According to the Belgian Georges Lemaitre (c. 1927), that dense pocket of gases resisted tremendous pressure exerted upon it, erupting with indescribable energy, causing the coherence of gases and dust into solids and initiating an interminable recessive movement in the universe. It is suggested that the "cooling off" period and subsequent stages in development of the earth, as part of that cosmic phenomenon, transpired over billions of years, accounting for diversity of geologic formations and fossilization during those elastic but clearly distinguishable epochs.

This purport of natural science may be accommodated by interpreting the "days" of the creative account in Genesis 1, not as literal twenty-four hour days, but as protracted periods of geologic development in the history of the earth. Indeed, the

Hebrew word for "day," *yom,* is a versatile term,[2] used in the Old Testament for the duration of a working day (Exodus 20:9, 10), the aggregate of generations (Psalm 90:10), the extent of regal reign (1 Kings 2:11), and a protracted period in a nation's history (Joel 2:1, 2). There is, therefore, sufficient precedent for rendering "day" in Genesis 1 other than a twenty-four hour span. It is interesting to note that traces of such an explanation of the record of creation are found in ancient Christian literature as early as the time of Augustine (c. 400),[3] doing no violence to *ex nihilo* ("out of nothing") intimations in Genesis 1:1 and Hebrews 11: 3.

But, while the earth may be of some immense age, it is more certain that man is not. Man is, comparatively, of rather recent introduction.[4] And, while naturalism and supernaturalism may enjoy some correspondence in matters of cosmic beginnings, they remain estranged as to the origin of man.

On the Origin of Man

Naturalism asserts that all life has evolved from a simple cell to more complex forms. It maintains that no species is fixed and changeless, and that only those species most fit and capable of adaptation have survived. Man, furthermore, was not "created" independently of the other animals, but is the present

---

2 See Francis Brown, S. R. Driver, and Charles A. Briggs, *A Hebrew and English Lexicon of the Old Testament* (Oxford: Oxford University Press, 1907), pp. 398-401.

3 *E.g., De Civitate Dei,* xi. 6, 8, 33, xii. 16; *De Genesi ad Litteram,* iii. 26, v. 3.

4 Many responsible evangelical scholars locate the advent of man c. B.C. 10,000-25,000, only coincidentally with the emergence of the alleged Cro-magnon of naturalistic supposition. Cf. Edward J. Carnell, Bernard Ramm, Merrill F. Unger, *et. al.*

vindication of evolutionary ascendancy. Insisting upon man's necessary linkage with an apelike ancestor, atheistic evolution makes no attempt to indicate a definite time at which the last step in the process was taken. Nor does it account for the appearance of the first life.[5]

Theistic evolution has tried to bridge the gulf between naturalism and supernaturalism by urging evolution as God's fixed mode of working. But this posture is contradictory to the teaching of Genesis 1, where each order of life is described as being created immediately and independently, bringing forth "after his kind." Theistic evolution, with its symbolic interpretation and mediate creationism, impugns the character of God and raises serious questions as to the veracity of the written Word.

Supernaturalism affirms that God created man from the dust of the ground, breathing into him the breath of life (Genesis 2:7). This accounts for material and immaterial natures. Only such a conception of the origin of man grants him dignity of being and responsibility of assignment, thus laying the foundation for a rational system of ethics and redemption.

In relating these difficult matters and placing a judgment upon them, the Christian is responsible for evaluating all the evidence at his disposal. He must assume a stance at once consistent with the Scriptures, yet cognizant and appreciative of the facts—but not the speculations—of natural science.

---

5 Atheistic evolution is at least as old as the Greek philosopher Anaximander (c. B.C. 575). Its most refined explications were offered by Jean Baptiste Lamarck (France, c. 1775) and Charles Darwin (England, c. 1860).

Erich Sauer well expresses an acceptable synthesis:

> . . . The whole development is one uniform con-
> tinued sequence, . . . one single colossal process,
> distributed over immense creative periods. In this
> . . . there came a gradual ascent in the forms of
> life. Finally man, *without* connexion by descent with
> the animal world, was placed on the stage of world
> events, in order to set out on his earthly course
> from the garden of Paradise expressly prepared for
> him.[6]

MAN IN THE "IMAGE OF GOD"

"And God said, Let us make man in our image,
after our likeness . . ." (Genesis 1:26). Thus Moses
reports that the idea and fact of man issued from
divine and eternal counsels. "So God created man in
his own image, in the image of God created he him"
(Genesis 1:27). In so simple and positive fashion
the inspired writer represents man's original estate.
There seems to be no appreciable difference between
the Hebrew words *tselem* ("image") and *demuth*
("likeness"); but the juxtaposition of the terms is
more an instance of a deliberate and varied redun-
dance characteristic of Semitic idiom. It is important,
however, to inquire in what that "image" or "likeness" consisted.

The Essential Spirituality of God

God is essentially a spiritual being. The "image
of God" after which man was created was itself a
spiritual image. In John 4:24 our Lord Himself announced the elemental truth respecting the nature
of God: "God is a Spirit: and they that worship him

---

6 Erich Sauer, *The Dawn of World Redemption; A Survey of Historical Revelation in the Old Testament*, trans. G. H. Lang (Grand
Rapids, Michigan: Wm. B. Eerdmans Publishing Company, 1955), p. 36.

must worship him in spirit and in truth." Jesus intended to impress upon us the marvelous realization that there is a part of our nature—the immaterial or spiritual—corresponding to the essential nature of God Himself. True worship is effected only when those properties are established in
divine-human reciprocity.

The essential spiritual body of God is consistent
both with His attribute of omnipresence (Psalm 139)
and with His commandment against making "any
graven image, or any likeness" of Him (Exodus 20:
4). It is in no way violated by His various self-
manifestations in the Old Testament. It is very
clear, of course, that God did on occasion appear in
tangible form in accordance with divine discretion.
Moses, for example, saw the "back parts" of God
(Exodus 33:23); Joshua was instructed by the "cap-
tain of the host of the Lord" (Joshua 5:
14); Nebuchadnezzar witnessed a fourth man in the
fiery furnace, "like the Son of God" (Daniel 3:25).
Appearances of this kind are called theophanies
("God-voice"), i.e., God's expression of Himself in
ways that man could tangibly discern. Such assump-
tions of bodily form, in themselves displays of divine grace whereby He who is spirit accommodated
the necessary limitations of eyes of flesh, enhance
rather than frustrate our attempts to understand
John 1:18: "No man hath seen God at any time. . . ."
Our Lord again affirms the spirituality of God: none
has ever seen Him as He essentially is, i.e., spirit.
(Cf. John 1:14.)

Nor do those scriptures apparently alluding to
bodily parts of God invalidate that essential spirituality. When the Bible speaks of the eyes, ears,

and arms of God, for example, the intention is to establish, not a physique analogous to man, but rather the method of divine operation. God's "eyes . . . upon the righteous" (Psalm 34:15) means that He is eternally aware of the proceedings of His children; God's "ears . . . open unto their cry" (Psalm 34:15) indicates His consciousness of their need for sustenance; God's "mighty arm" (Psalm 89:13) connotes an omnipotence of the Creator over all the circumstances of the creation. These are instances of anthropomorphism ("man-form"), figures of speech whereby familiar language is employed to describe an otherwise indescribable God. Anthropomorphism illustrates the works of God, not the essential nature of deity.

The Corresponding Endowment of Man

Since God is incomprehensible and in all points cannot be fully explained with reference to His spiritual form, we may conclude that this image at its very least is a mental, moral and social likeness. Charles Hodge states:

> God is a Spirit, the human soul is a spirit. The essential attributes of a spirit are reason, conscience, and will. A spirit is a rational, moral, and therefore also, a free agent. In making man after his own image, therefore, God endowed him with those attributes which belong to his own nature as a spirit. Man is thereby distinguished from all other inhabitants of this world, and raised immeasurably above them. He belongs to the same order of being as God Himself, and is therefore capable of communion with his Maker. This conformity of nature between man and God . . . is also the necessary condition of our capacity to know God, and therefore the foundation of our religious nature. If we

were not like God, we could not know Him. We
should be as the beasts which perish.[7]

In so commenting on the mental aspect of this likeness, Hodge is but confirming the Pauline assertion
of man's being "renewed in knowledge after the
image of him that created him" (Colossians 3:10).
This renewal begins in regeneration and is continued in sanctification. Man's endowment with
substantial intellectual faculties is implied in the
commands that he tend the garden (Genesis 2:15)
and exercise dominion over all the other creatures
of the earth (Genesis 1:26, 28, 2:19, 20). And

> this likeness to God is inalienable, and since it
> constitutes man's capacity for redemption, it gives
> value to the life even of the unregenerated. . . .
> [See Genesis 9:6; James 3:9, 10.] How different
> is this conception of the original condition of man
> from that of the evolutionist, who thinks of the first
> man as only a shade above the brute, not only
> ignorant, but with practically no mental ability
> whatever![8]

That man has a moral likeness to God is also a
Pauline tenet. In regeneration the new man "after
God is created in righteousness and true holiness"
(Ephesians 4:24). It is undoubtedly correct, therefore, to infer that man in his primitive estate had
both righteousness and holiness. Only upon such
condition was it possible for him to have communion
with God. Genesis 1:31 reports that "God saw every
thing that he had made, and, behold, it was very

---

7 Charles Hodge, *Systematic Theology* (Grand Rapids, Michigan:
Wm. B. Eerdmans Publishing Company, 1952), II, 96-7.

8 Henry C. Thiessen, *Introductory Lectures in Systematic Theology*
(Grand Rapids, Michigan: Wm. B. Eerdmans Publishing Company, 1949),
p. 220.

good." This includes man, and would not have been true if he had been morally deficient. It is important, furthermore, to notice that man possessed the divine image by the very fact of his creation, not by some subsequent bestowal of it. It is inadequate to say that the creature was fashioned in a state of innocence. "Holiness is more than innocence. . . . Man was made not only negatively innocent, but positively holy." [9]

The social likeness of God after which man has been created accounts for human love and societal interests prevailing in spite of the fall. As God's social nature, grounded in His affections, finds the objects of His love in the Trinity, so man seeks a fellowship with his own kind (Genesis 2:18, 11:1, 9). This desire for fellowship provided a rationale for the pursuit of the corporate good and for the potential redemption of the larger social whole.

THE UNITY AND PERMANENT CONSTITUTION OF MAN

All men are children of a common parentage. The Scriptures clearly teach that the whole race is descended from a single pair. God told the male and female that He had created to "be fruitful, and multiply, and replenish the earth, and subdue it . . ." (Genesis 1:28).[10] Adam, therefore, "called his wife's name Eve; because she was the mother of all living" (Genesis 3:20).

---

9 Wm. G. T. Shedd, *Dogmatic Theology* (New York: Charles Scribner's Sons, 1889), II, 96.

10 This verse has often been used to lend substance to speculation concerning a pre-Adamic race. "Replenish," implying "fill up *again*," is an unfortunate translation here. The Hebrew *male'* means simply "plenish," or "fill up," intimating neither antecedence nor repetition.

His Solidarity Attested

This truth is assumed in the Pauline doctrine of the organic unity of mankind in the first transgression and of the provision of salvation for those in Christ: "Wherefore, as by one man sin entered into the world, and death by sin; and so death passed upon all men, for that all have sinned. . . . For as by one man's disobedience many were made sinners, so by the obedience of one shall many be made righteous" (Romans 5:12, 19); "For since by man came death, by man came also the resurrection of the dead. For as in Adam all die, so in Christ shall all be made alive" (1 Corinthians 15:21, 22). This truth also constitutes the ground of man's responsibility toward his fellow-man: "And [God] hath made of one blood all nations of men for to dwell on all the face of the earth . . ." (Acts 17:26; cf. Genesis 4:9, 10).

A gratifying array of scientific evidence corroborates the biblical teaching of the unity of the race. History traces the lines of tribes and nations in both hemispheres to a common ancestry in central Asia; comparative philology points to a common source for all the more important languages of mankind; physiology, in affirming functional commonality, admits only one species of man; psychology attests common mental and moral characteristics among all families of mankind, as evidenced in common maxims, tendencies, and capacities and in the prevalence of similar traditions.[11] The sciences, then, complement divine revelation in certifying the soli-

---

11 See Hodge, *op. cit.*, II, 77-91; Thiessen, *op. cit.*, pp. 223-5. Cf. George P. Fisher, *The Grounds of Theistic and Christian Belief* (New York: Charles Scribner's Sons, 1897), pp. 469-83.

darity of the race. All varieties of men are of one species, a matter once again of urgent import respecting the scope and intent of the plan of redemption.

His Nature Described

The unity of mankind thus established allows for ascertaining the constitution of the individual representative. Genesis 2:7 tells us that man consists of two distinct principles, one material and the other immaterial, or one corporeal and the other spiritual. His former was fashioned from the dust of the ground, his latter infused, so that when God dispensed the "breath of life," "man became a living soul [nephesh]." The immaterial nature is composed of two parts. Sometimes the parts are sharply distinguished; at other times they stand for the whole being. Paul carefully delineates between body (material) and soul and spirit (immaterial) in 1 Thessalonians 5:23 (cf. Hebrews 4:12). This teaching of the divisibility of man's immaterial nature, rendering him of tripartite constitution, is called trichotomy.

Human nature is the sum of those forces which render man what he is. The body (soma) is the instrument whereby intelligent and willful exercises are pursued. Two particular events—one past, the other future—assign it great dignity. By incarnation God in Christ took a body like ours; in resurrection we shall take a glorified body like His. Soul (psuche) may be defined as the living being, the principle of animal (social-conscious) life, with which are associated the emotions, interests, and inclinations. Spirit (pneuma) means that which is the mark of the living as opposed to the dead. It is the motive force of the soul, God-conscious and productive of rational and volitional capabilities. The corporeal principle of man returns at death to the dust from which it came, to await its resurrection, while the spiritual principle is reserved for God's judgment; the corporeal may become disorganized, dispersed, or apparently annihilated, but the spiritual persists in conscious life and activity.[12]

The whole range of man's faculties was affected by the fall, necessitating urgent and radical redemption. What were the intricate ramifications of original sin? In order to understand the redemptive provision, it is necessary first to discuss the human predicament.

SUMMARY QUESTIONS

1. Define: anthropology, *ex nihilo,* theophany, anthropomorphism, trichotomy.

2. What are the basic differences between naturalism and supernaturalism?

3. What are the fallacies of theistic evolution?

4. In what does the "image of God" in man consist?

5. What are some evidences of the organic unity of the race?

---

12 Alan Richardson (ed.), *A Theological Wordbook of the Bible* (New York: The Macmillan Company, 1950), pp. 144-6. Cf. Hodge, *op. cit.,* II, 42-4, 54-5.

2

The Fall of Man

In commenting on the "dust of the ground" (Genesis 2:7) from which the creature's material principle was fashioned, H. C. Leupold suggests that

> lest man form too high an estimate of the first man, it is here recorded that, in spite of the high station involved in being made in the image of God, man has a constituent part in his makeup, which forever forbids unseemly pride on his part—a thought frequently stressed in the devotional literature of the church, from days of old. Without this fact to reckon with we could hardly have been in a position to understand how a temptation and fall were even possible. Practically everything written in chapter two [of Genesis] definitely paves the way for chapter three.[1]

Temptation and fall in Genesis 3 are those pivotal events around which the sacred writer has chosen to construct his historical narrative in explication of sin's entrance into the world. But that account is better understood against the background of certain philosophical antecedents.

---

1 H. C. Leupold, *Exposition of Genesis* (Grand Rapids, Michigan: Baker Book House, 1942), I, 115-6.

THE ORIGIN AND NATURE OF SIN

Christian faith affirms that Almighty God created the world out of nothing by free, sovereign power, and presently directs the movement of history according to the counsels of His own will, to the ultimate display of His infinite perfection and glory and the salvation of many through grace merited by the redemptive work of His Son. If God is the Author of everything, then He may rightfully be called to account for the present state of affairs. Traditionally, the assignment of relating a universe replete with evil to the Author of that universe, who is supposed to be wholly good, is known as the problem of evil.

Evil has been defined as anything that frustrates human values. Basically, there are two kinds of evil —natural and moral. Natural evil includes those frustrations perpetrated by natural elements in the universe, such as disease of the body, fury of hurricane, and even death itself. Moral evil (sin) embraces those frustrations perpetrated by the free agency of man, such as materialism, militarism, and bigotry. Such seem clearly to contradict the Christian hypothesis that the universe was created by a benevolent God.

Philosophical Considerations

The really intricate nature of the problem of evil may be stated concisely in terms of four alternative propositions: (1) either God wants to prevent evil, and cannot; or, (2) He can prevent it, and does not want to; or, (3) He neither wants to nor can prevent it; or (4) He wants to and can prevent it. If God has the desire without the power, He is impotent; if He can, but has not the desire, He is malicious; if he has neither the power nor the desire, he is both impotent and malicious; if He has the desire and the power, then what is the source of evil, and why does He not prevent it? It is clear that, in keeping with the final proposition, to leave the matter of evil as mystery is inadequate in view of the assertions that Christianity is systematically consistent.

Edward John Carnell insists that there are only three alternative choices in solution to the problem of evil.[2] The first is the disposal of evil by denial of its true reality. Pantheism, for example, which defines God as all (*i.e.*, nature and God are continuous) and all as God, makes evil illusory. Christian Science, also, with its rejection of the reality of pain, is a philosophy of illusion. That evil does exist, however, is attested by abundant empirical evidence; nor does this postulation actually solve the problem of evil. To the contrary, it makes incumbent upon its advocate the accounting for the reality of the illusion.

A second choice is to admit that both evil and God are real, and that the two are co-eternal principles. Dualistic approaches have taken many forms in the history of philosophy. Platonism, Zoroastrianism, and Manichaeism all suggested that there is more than one ultimate principle of reality. Dualism is unsatisfying, however, for it makes God finite and offers no hope that the eternal con-

---

2 Edward John Carnell, *An Introduction to Christian Apologetics; A Philosophic Defense of the Trinitarian-Theistic Faith* (Grand Rapids, Michigan: Wm. B. Eerdmans Publishing Company, 1948), pp. 283ff.

flict between good and evil will ever be resolved. If not, what prospect is there of immortality?

Christian theism is the only tenable answer to the problem of evil. It maintains that a sovereign God decreed the present universe, willfully permitting the entrance of evil into it to fulfill those purposes which were elected in His own eternal counsels. This position not only satisfies those questions attending the beginning and the consummation of history, but renders history some rationality in its total progress. As Albert Outler has stated in his *Who Trusts in God: Musings on the Meaning of Providence,* God's providence in history (teleology) is neither as a meddling director nor yet as an absentee landlord, but rather as history's assessor, providing those meanings and purposes that are worthily human and guaranteeing, against all odds, the eventual triumph of righteousness. [3]

Christian theism, furthermore, in sustaining the sovereignty and integrity of God, puts squarely upon the creature the responsibility for all the sin and sorrow which comprise both natural and moral evil, for angel and man brought disruption into this perfect universe through their defection from the divine commands. That defection and its results constitutes the burden of Genesis 3.

Biblical Considerations

In language conspicuous for the absence of

---

3 Albert C. Outler, *Who Trusts in God: Musings on the Meaning of Providence* (New York: Oxford University Press, 1968), p. 80. Cf. Romans 8:28, where the best Greek text reads: "And we know that God works all things together for good. . . ."

technical vocabulary, Moses reports that episode supremely affecting the whole destiny of the race:

> Now the serpent was more subtil than any beast of the field which the Lord God had made. And he said unto the woman, Yea, hath God said, Ye shall not eat of every tree of the garden? And the woman said unto the serpent, We may eat of the fruit of the trees of the garden: But of the fruit of the tree which is in the midst of the garden, God hath said, Ye shall not eat of it, neither shall ye touch it, lest ye die. And the serpent said unto the woman, Ye shall not surely die: For God doth know that in the day ye eat thereof, then your eyes shall be opened, and ye shall be as gods, knowing good and evil. And when the woman saw that the tree was good for food, and that it was pleasant to the eyes, and a tree to be desired to make one wise, she took of the fruit thereof, and did eat, and gave also unto her husband with her; and he did eat. And the eyes of them both were opened, and they knew that they were naked; and they sewed fig leaves together, and made themselves aprons. And they heard the voice of the Lord God walking in the garden in the cool of the day: and Adam and his wife hid themselves from the presence of the Lord God amongst the trees of the garden. (Genesis 3:1-8)

A prohibition, sharpened by reference to serious consequences, unequivocally expressed the will of God for man. Since the authority of deity would seem to be beyond human assault, this remained, at first, inviolate. Only the clever serpent (*i.e.*, Satan, using the serpent as his material instrument) perceived this disproportion between the seriousness of the consequences and the apparent triviality of the forbidden action. In order to initiate discussion, the serpent posed to the woman a leading question as to the scope of the prohibition, proceeding thereafter to entice her to renounce her literal conception of it. The thesis of the serpent was that the warning of God was not to be taken seriously— that God aimed, for His own interests, to restrain the woman by fear from something which she might easily take by transgression of the command.

Already attracted by the external appearance of the forbidden fruit, the woman yielded to the temptation to partake. The man, present with the woman, participated in her action, arrested by those prospects of wisdom and power intimated by the serpent. In that fatal chain of events emphasis obviously falls upon the lie that they shall "be as gods, knowing good and evil." It may be added that any man begins to "be like God" when, through that first doubt, he concedes that divine strictures are not in his interests and that the divine will may, at his own option, be countermanded. Reference is usually made to that garden experience as the "original sin." [4]

But how could a holy being sin? Certain preclusions must be made before a positive attempt at response is offered: God did not put motives before

---

4 This study cannot include a detailed presentation of Satan and the origin of sin in the universe. It is clear, however, that he (formerly the angel Lucifer, "light-bearer") had fallen from his high estate prior to the drama in the garden. Some suggest his expulsion from heaven to have occurred between Genesis 1:1 and 1:2, thus causing a universal catastrophe that rendered the earth "without form, and void." Others prefer simply to locate that event at some undetermined time before Genesis 3.

Satan is, at any rate, and as his very name implies, the "adversary" of God and the antagonist of His will. The Bible offers no explicit Satanology, although he is called the "prince of the power of the air" (Ephesians 2:2), who, "as a roaring lion, walketh about, seeking whom he may devour" (1 Peter 5:8). At this point the Christian philosophy takes a new dimension concerning the problem of evil: evil is no mere abstraction, nor only a necessary defect in the good (as Augustine), but a person.

man that led him to sin—that would make God
responsible and absolve man of guilt; God did not
remove from man His sustaining grace—that would
likewise charge God with responsibility; the power
of choice with which God endowed man did not inevitably result in sin, for mere power of choice
does not explain the fact of an unholy choice. Although no answer to this difficult question is without its weaknesses, we may approximate the truth
by positing that man fell by a wrong use of free will.

> . . . Sin originated in man's free act of revolt
> from God—the act of a will which, though inclined
> toward God, was not yet confirmed in virtue and
> was still capable of a contrary choice. The original
> possession of such power to the contrary seems to
> be the necessary condition of probation and moral
> development. Yet the exercise of this power in a
> sinful direction can never be explained upon
> grounds of reason, since sin is essentially unreason.
> It is an act of wicked arbitrariness, the only motive
> of which is the desire to depart from God and to
> render self supreme.[5]

According to the progress of Genesis 3:1-8, that
wrong use of free will proceeded from the following
considerations of the nature of sin:

(1) Sin is an improper attitude toward God's
specific law ("Yea, hath God said . . . ?");

(2) Sin is a posture of self-sufficiency apart from
God ("Ye shall not surely die");

---

[5] Augustus Hopkins Strong, *Systematic Theology* (Philadelphia: The
Judson Press, 1907), p. 587. Cf. Hubert P. Black, "The Problem of
Evil," *Christianity Today*, XV (April 23, 1971), 12: ". . . Moral evil
results from an intelligent choice of defection." Note that this view
rejects the Gnostic tenet that sin originates in sensuousness. Finitude
itself is no sin, although one may yield his members as instruments
of sin (Romans 6:12-14).

(3) Sin is a desire for independence from God ("Your eyes shall be opened, and ye shall be as gods, knowing . . .");

(4) Sin is the centering of the self upon something or someone less than God ("The woman saw that the tree was . . . pleasant to the eyes, and . . . to be desired");

(5) Sin is the placing of selfish interests before God ("The woman saw that the tree was good for food");

(6) Sin is a voluntary, willful disobedience ("She took of the fruit . . . and did eat");

(7) Sin is a contagion ("She . . . gave also unto her husband with her");

(8) Sin is an estrangement from God ("Adam and his wife hid themselves from the presence of the Lord God").

The Apostle John, as if in retrospect upon the Genesis account, summarizes the nature of sin as "the lust of the flesh, and the lust of the eyes, and the pride of life" (1 John 2:16).

Linguistic Considerations

That separation of man from God wrought by sin in the garden is attested by the literal meanings of the several designations for sin in the Scriptures. Among the most frequently employed in the Hebrew Old Testament are the following:[6]

---

6 See Francis Brown, S. R. Driver, and Charles A. Briggs, *A Hebrew and English Lexicon of the Old Testament* (Oxford: Oxford University Press, 1907), pp. 306-8, 730-1, 833, 957; and Alan Richardson (ed.), *A Theological Wordbook of the Bible* (New York: The Macmillan Company, 1950), pp. 226-8.

(1) *Hata'*, "to sin." First found in Genesis 4:7, this verb is defined as "to miss the mark" (Judges 20:16) or "to miss the step" (Proverbs 19:2). Thus it means to miss or deviate from the goal prescribed by God for man. In its root meaning, *hata'* refers to action and not to estate.

(2.) *'Awon*, "iniquity." Sometimes interchangeable with the noun form of *hata'*, *'awon* indicates "to be bent, crooked." This word stipulates a perversion of the divine law, then the guilt of that course (Genesis 15:16). It denotes, primarily, the character of an action (1 Samuel 20:30; 2 Samuel 19:19).

(3) *Pasha'*, "transgression." This noun, like *'awon*, often stands for the noun form of *hata'*, and refers to "a breach" with God, hence "rebellion" and "apostasy." Whereas the noun form of *hata'* includes sins of negligence and weakness, *pasha'* indicates sins of deliberate design or set purpose (1 Kings 12:19; Isaiah 43:27).

(4) *Rasha'*, "wickedness, ungodliness." The opposite of righteousness, this noun represents the restless activity of the fallen nature. It signifies an habitual feature of disposition and action (Deuteronomy 9:27; Isaiah 58:4).

The New Testament, as well, is rich in a variety of Greek terms illustrating the nature of sin. Those words most widely used include: [7]

---

7 See William F. Arndt and F. Wilbur Gingrich, *A Greek-English Lexicon of the New Testament and Other Early Christian Literature* (Chicago: University of Chicago Press, 1957), pp. 41-3, 114, 617, 697; and Gerhard Kittel (ed.), *Theological Dictionary of the New Testament*, trans. Geoffrey W. Bromiley (Grand Rapids, Michigan: Wm. B. Eerdmans Publishing Company, 1964-   ), I, 267-316, V, 739-40, VI, 562-6.

(1) *Hamartano,* "to sin." This verb means "to miss the mark," and refers to sin, whether it occurs by omission or commission, in thought, feeling, speech, or action (Titus 3:11; 2 Peter 2:4).

(2) *Ponaria,* "perversion, maliciousness, iniquity." *Ponaria* identifies the active exercise of a vicious disposition. This noun may be rendered "evil-mindedness," signifying wicked purposes and desires (Mark 7:22; Romans 1:29).

(3) *Parabasis,* "transgression." Indicating "a going over," the noun *parabasis,* like *anomia* ("lawlessness"), refers to the absolute breach of a definite, promulgated, ratified law. It bespeaks an intentional act, whereas the noun form of *hamartano* may be a sin of ignorance or negligence (Romans 2:23, 5:14).

(4) *Asebeia,* "wickedness, ungodliness." A noun depicting a basic want of reverence toward God, *asebeia* is used especially of profligate and heathen impiety (Romans 1:18; 2 Timothy 2:16).

Behind this representative diversity of derivation of Old and New Testament words there lies a fundamental, unified conception of sin characterized in part as failure, in part as irregularity or crookedness, and in part as infringement upon the psychic totality of man. Sinful actions are viewed as preying upon the positive forces of life; divine law is transgressed because the soul itself is diseased. More deep-seated sin spreads like poison, issues in violence and mischief, is allied with a curse as righteousness is identified with blessing, and finally must destroy the offender.

Consider, furthermore, the power of sin so graphically illustrated in these verses: sin "lieth [croucheth]" at the door (Genesis 4:7); sin will "find [search] you out" (Numbers 32:23); sin is "deceitfulness" (Hebrews 3:13; cf. Job 20:12-14); sin so easily "besets [surrounds, ambushes] us" (Hebrews 12:1); sin takes captive and holds with "cords" (Proverbs 5:22); sin will "testify" in a judicial way (Isaiah 59:12); sin has a "sting of death" administered by Satan (1 Corinthians 15:55, 56; cf. Hebrews 2:14); sin will "slay" in the end (Psalm 34: 21).

THE UNIVERSAL IMPUTATION OF SIN

Throughout the Scriptures the teaching prevails that not only Adam and Eve, but also the entire race of which they were the progenitors, suffers because of sin. As they were corrupted, so their posterity share not only in that moral deficiency but also in the guilt of original transgression.

The Fact of Imputation

Assertions to this effect are numerous. Some from the Old Testament follow:

"There is no man that sinneth not" (1 Kings 8: 46); "Behold, I was shapen in iniquity; and in sin did my mother conceive me" (Psalm 51:5); "If thou, Lord, shouldest mark iniquities, O Lord, who shall stand?" (Psalm 130:3); "In thy sight shall no man living be justified" (Psalm 143:2; better, "In thy sight no man living is righteous"); "Who can say, I have made my heart clean, I am pure from my sin?" (Proverbs 20:9); "For there is not a just man upon earth, that doeth good, and sinneth not" (Ecclesiastes 7:20); "All we like sheep have gone astray; we have turned every one to his own way" (Isaiah 53:6); "We are all as an unclean thing, and all our righteousnesses are as filthy rags" (Isaiah 64:6).

The New Testament, furthermore, states: "There is none righteous, no, not one" (Romans 3:10); "All the world . . . guilty before God. Therefore by the deeds of the law there shall no flesh be justified in his sight" (Romans 3:19, 20); "All have sinned, and come short of the glory of God" (Romans 3:23); "The Scripture hath concluded [shut up] all under sin" (Galatians 3:22); "If we say that we have no sin, we deceive ourselves, and the truth is not in us" (1 John 1:8); "The whole world lieth in wickedness [the evil one]" (1 John 5:19).

It is clear that the controlling power of sin is everywhere evident in the annals of human experience, and its early manifestations well established. The present state of human nature is not its normal and original condition. We are a fallen race. A formidable foe, then, sin wrought consequences in Eden that affect us today no less.

The Consequences of Imputation

Those results, both immediate and remote in range, touch material as well as immaterial properties:

One of the consequences of Adam's sin was physical death. All men must die, and death is, according to the Scriptures, a penal evil. Death, including the prospect of physical and mental illness because of a general vulnerability, presupposes sin; no rational, moral creature is subject to expiration except on account of it. Immediately after his original transgression, Adam was told by God that "dust thou art, and unto dust shalt thou return" (Genesis 3:19). And the Hebrew of Genesis 2:17 may well be translated as "dying thou shalt die," so that man became a dying creature from the instant of that initial violation of the divine word and will.

Another effect of Adam's sin was a curse upon his environment. Animal creation was an object of God's curse (Genesis 3:14); but in a distant age it will be removed (Isaiah 11:6-9). The earth was also placed under a curse (Genesis 3:17, 18) and now "groaneth" and "travaileth in pain" together with the creature, until the day of future redemption (Romans 8:21, 22; cf. Isaiah 35). It was a hostile environment, therefore, to which Adam and Eve were consigned (Genesis 3:22-24).

But the severest penalty of the Adamic transgression was spiritual death. Whereas physical death was the prospect of separation of soul from body, spiritual death entails separation of the soul from God. This dimension of the penal consequence involves three distinct but related elements in causal succession: *depravity, inability, guilt.*

Depravity, from the negative standpoint, is man's want of original righteousness and holy affections toward God; positively, it is the corruption of his moral nature and bias toward evil. Not every sinner is devoid of all those qualities pleasing to men, nor is he prone to commit every form of sin and to stand in all possible bitter opposition to God. But he is destitute of that love to God which is the fundamental requirement of the law (Deuteronomy 6:4, 5; Matthew 22:35-38); he is supremely given to a preference of himself to God (2 Timothy 3:4); he has an aversion to God which on occasion becomes active enmity against Him (Romans 8:7); he is disordered and corrupted in every faculty (Ephesians 4:18); he has no thought, feeling, or deed of which God can fully approve (Romans 7:18); and he has entered upon a course of constant progress in depravity, from which he himself is utterly powerless to turn away.

But, while depravity has produced in the sinner a total spiritual inability in the sense that he cannot by his own volition change his character and life so as to make them conformable to the law of God, there yet remains a power of choice fully compatible with the complete bondage of his will in spiritual things. Inability consists not in the loss of any faculty of the soul, nor in the loss of free agency, but in want of spiritual discernment and of proper affections issuing therefrom. Thus, depravity renders man unable to love and serve God as he ought, and that very inability incurs the guilt of "missing the mark." [8]

The Representative Principle

Imputation of sin is a fundamental tenet of the Scriptures, but they elaborate more the fact than the method of that assignment. In the theological sense, to impute *(logidzomai,* "to charge to the account of") is to attribute anything to a person or persons upon adequate grounds, such as the judicial or meritorious reason of reward or punishment. To impute

---

[8] See Charles Hodge, *Systematic Theology* (Grand Rapids, Michigan: Wm. B. Eerdmans Publishing Company, 1952), II, 186-92, 254-64; and Henry C. Thiessen, *Introductory Lectures in Systematic Theology* (Grand Rapids, Michigan: Wm. B. Eerdmans Publishing Company, 1949), pp. 267-72.

sin means to impute the guilt of sin, *i.e.*, the judicial obligation to satisfy divine justice. The ground of the imputation of Adam's sin is the union between him and his posterity, a union both natural and federal. That such was the relationship is unmistakable from the Genesis narrative. Everything there said to Adam was communicated to him in his capacity as representative man. The promise of life, the charge to dominion, the warning against disobedience—through a covenant of works all belonged to his descendants as well as to himself alone.

This representative principle pervades the Scriptures, so that the imputation of Adam's sin to his posterity is not an isolated fact. (Cf. the histories of Canaan, Esau, Eli, *et. al.*) The parallel drawn by the Apostle Paul is the major case in point. To Paul, Adam was the type of Him who was to come, because as the one was representative of his race, so the Other is representative of His people. And the consequences of that relationship are analogous: as Adam was the representative of his race, and his sin is the judicial ground of its condemnation, so Christ is the representative of His people and His righteousness the judicial ground of their justification. Men are both condemned and justified by actions not personally their own. [9]

Immediate imputation is taught most precisely in Romans 5:12-21. Verses 12 and 17-19 carry the burden of his message:

Wherefore, as by one man sin entered into the

---

9 See Hodge, *op. cit.*, II, 192-205. It is interesting, furthermore, to note the indication of solidarity of the race in Romans 3:23. The Greek reads, "for all *sinned* [*hamarton*]," as if the Apostle were reflecting upon a single historical event.

world, and death by sin; and so death passed upon
all men, for that all have sinned: . . . For if by one
man's offence death reigned by one; much more
they which receive abundance of grace and of the
gift of righteousness shall reign in life by one,
Jesus Christ. Therefore as by the offence of one
judgment came upon all men to condemnation;
even so by the righteousness of one the free gift
came upon all men unto justification of life. For
as by one man's disobedience many were made sinners, so by the obedience of one shall many be made
righteous.

This agrees not only with the Mosaic account of the
fall, but also with the Apostle's subsequent teaching
in 1 Corinthians 15:21, 22: "For since by man came
death, by man came also the resurrection of the dead.
For as in Adam all die, even so in Christ shall all be
made alive." Union with Adam is the cause of
death; union with Christ is the cause of life.[10]

---

10 Several divergent views have been taken in the history of the
Christian Church respecting the method of imputation:

(1) The Pelagian Theory. Pelagius, a British monk (c. 400), suggested man's natural innocence, admitting the possibility that one
can consistently choose the good, i.e., never sin. In effect, this is a view
of non-imputation, for Adam injured only himself.

(2) The Arminian Theory. Jacob Arminius (Holland, c. 1600) taught
a voluntarily appropriated depravity. Like Pelagius, Arminius rejected
the innate depravity of man; but unlike Pelagius, he believed that all
men would inevitably sin. Man becomes a sinner only when that first
wrong choice is made. This view has been called Semi-Pelagianism.

(3) The Mediate Theory. Placeus (France, c. 1600) projected that
physical depravity descended by natural propagation from Adam, and
that the soul, created and allocated by God to each individual, becomes
corrupt upon union with the body.

(4) The Augustinian Theory. In opposition to Pelagianism, Augustine
(c. 400) insisted that God imputes the sin of Adam immediately to all
his posterity by virtue of the seminal relationship in which they stand.
This view includes the teaching of traducianism—that the soul as well
as the body is transmitted from Adam.

It may be added that the Federal Theory, commended in the text
above, seems to have originated with Cocceius (Holland, c. 1650). As
to the soul's origin, this covenant view tends towards creationism, and
usually assigns the method of imputation as by legal or forensic
decree of God.

THE RESULTANT CHARACTER OF MAN

One eminent historical document of the Christian Church gives adequate summarization of preceding discussion: "The sinfulness of that estate whereinto man fell, consists in, the guilt of Adam's first sin, the want of original righteousness, and the corruption of his whole nature, which is commonly called original sin; together with all actual transgressions which proceed from it." By their fall, it continues, all mankind "lost communion with God, are under his wrath and curse, and so made liable to all the miseries of this life, to death itself, and to the pains of hell forever."[11]

Man is constituted a sinner by *nature*, by *estate*, and by *act*. Resident corruption offends the holiness of God; protracted impotence flaunts the power of God; persistent infraction of divine law provokes the justice of God. Scripture and human experience alike attest man's miserable condition apart from redeeming and enabling grace. Materialism, militarism, bigotry, depersonalization, environmental pollution—all these in our own time have rendered null and void the tenuous optimism of theological liberalism. Dissatisfaction with that former philosophy, as evidenced by the contemporary rise of realism, is symptomatic in a very real sense of a return to that theology of depravity which conservative Christianity has always postulated as an integral element in its world view.[12]

Thus the image of God in man has been desper-

---

11 Westminster Shorter Catechism, Articles 18, 19.

12 Although we would not endorse all their tenets, it might be noted here that this change in theological direction constitutes in part the legacy of Karl Barth, Reinhold Niebuhr, and Dietrich Bonhoeffer.

ately marred. It has not been effaced, however, and that is what renders him redeemable. The history of that redemptive provision is a marvelous odyssey, and its circumstances a study in the progress of revelation.

SUMMARY QUESTIONS

1. Define: evil, providence, depravity, imputation, federal.
2. Why is Christian theism the only satisfactory answer to the problem of evil?
3. Discuss the nature of sin according to the progress of Genesis 3:1-8.
4. What does the Bible teach about the universality of sin?
5. What were the consequences of the "original sin"?

3

The Purpose of God

Soteriology refers to the doctrines of salvation. The term is derived from two Greek words, *soteria* ("salvation") and *logos* ("discourse"). Soteriology deals with the provision of salvation through Christ and the application of it through the Holy Spirit. Because it does concern redemption, restoration, and renewal, it can be understood only against the background of the original condition of man as created in the image of God, and of the subsequent disturbance of the proper relationship between man and his God by the entrance of sin into the world.

Treating the salvation of the sinner wholly as the work of God, moreover, known to Him from all eternity, soteriology naturally carries our thoughts back to the eternal counsel of peace and the covenant of grace, in which provision was made for the redemption of fallen man. The study proceeds on the assumption of the completed work of Christ as Mediator of redemption, effecting the closest possible connection between Christology and soteriology.

THE PURPOSE OF GOD IN HUMAN
NATURE: General Revelation

Communication of the blessings of salvation to the sinner and his restoration to divine favor and to a life in intimate fellowship with Himself has been the purpose of God in human nature no less than in the Scriptures. Man's fall occasioned the loss of his original innocence and holiness, but it did not deprive him of all spiritual knowledge. This remnant of understanding that God has allowed man to retain is recognized universally by all who engage in an investigation of men and their mores. Anthropologists and missionaries alike have reported consistently that every tribe of men, no matter how primitive, even that one which upon first contact appeared to have no religion, upon more careful scrutiny has been shown to sustain some conception of God. According to Romans 1:20, men have this knowledge on the testimony of the voice of creation (cf. Psalm 19:1-6); and on the basis of John 1:9, as John Wesley interpreted it, men have this knowledge from the witness of conscience. God has seen to it that a testimony to Himself should never completely disappear.

The knowledge of sin is as universal as the knowledge of God. Both are innate as well as acquired, and the former seems to be enhanced in direct proportion as the latter is enlarged. One of the most striking aspects of the universal religious community is its insistence upon the need of sacrifice for appeasement of deity and atonement for sins. It is significant that within this context of sacrifice the heathen are constrained to perform their rites from fear of their gods rather than from motivation to love and devotion. "This conviction of the need of a mediator (priest) and a work of mediation (sacrifice) adds to the evidence in favor of an indication of God's purpose to provide salvation for mankind."[1]

God's testimony to Himself in nature and in human nature is referred to as general revelation. By this means man knows that God *is*, but he does not know what *kind* of a God He is. That is the purpose of special revelation. Berkhof distinguishes between them this way:

> General revelation is rooted in creation, is addressed to man as man, and more particularly to human reason, and finds its purpose in the realization of the end of his creation, to know God and thus enjoy communion with Him. Special revelation is rooted in the redemptive plan of God, is addressed to man as a sinner, can be properly understood and appropriated only by faith, and serves the purpose of securing the end for which man was created in spite of the disturbance wrought by sin.[2]

"In view of the eternal plan of redemption," he adds, "it should be said that this special revelation did not come in as an after-thought, but was in the mind of God from the very beginning."[3]

THE PURPOSE OF GOD IN
THE SCRIPTURES: Special Revelation

Natural theology fails to communicate the truths

1 Henry C. Thiessen, *Introductory Lectures in Systematic Theology* (Grand Rapids, Michigan: Wm. B. Eerdmans Publishing Company, 1949), p. 276.

2 L. Berkhof, *Systematic Theology* (Grand Rapids, Michigan: Wm. B. Eerdmans Publishing Company, 1941), p. 37.

3 *Ibid.*

of salvation. Those are metaphysical in essence and must be conveyed by a gracious God in some unique way corresponding to His will. That He has established in His written Word. And He who works in an orderly fashion in nature has not left the salvation of man to careless and uncertain experimentation.

> Scripture shows us that He has a definite plan of salvation. This plan includes the means by which salvation is to be provided, the objectives that are to be realized, the persons that are to benefit by it, the conditions on which it is to be available, and the agents and means by which it is to be applied. It may be added that He has only one plan and that all must be saved in the same way, if they are to be saved at all, whether they be uncivilized or civilized, immoral or moral, whether living in the Old Testament dispensation or in the present age.[4]

It is clear, then, that the Scriptures must be studied as one whole revelation[5] if we would accurately discern the dimensions of His redemptive plan.

Augustine's famous dictum was *in Vetere Novum lateat, et in Novo Vetus pateat, i.e.,* "The New [Testament] is in the Old [Testament] concealed, and the Old [Testament] is in the New [Testament] revealed."[6] Since the New Testament, therefore, is the fulfillment and explanation of the Old, it is proper that we should turn principally to the Old for the disclosure of God's purpose. Throughout the whole of that sacred corpus, Jesus Christ is presented as Redeemer in the progress of revelation.

---

4 Thiessen, *op. cit.,* pp. 277-8.
5 The Greek word for "revelation" is *apokalupsis,* meaning "to have the veil or cover removed from." This is definitive of God's gracious action regarding the communication of divine truth to finite minds.
6 *Quaestionum in Heptateuchum,* II, 73.

The Progress of Revelation

There is a certain sacred irony in the fact that the first intimation of redemption should have occurred in the context of the divine curse upon the serpent, *i.e.*, Satan: "And I will put enmity between thee and the woman, and between thy seed and her seed; it shall bruise thy head, and thou shalt bruise his heel." Genesis 3:15[7] is known as the *protoevangelium*—the "foregospel" or "first good news." That the verse is clearly Messianic has been the position of the Jewish interpreters, of Paul (see Romans 16:20), of Irenaeus and other early Church Fathers, and of Luther and all other major Reformers.

Both the ultimate victory over Satan and the achievement of it by the seed of the woman are clearly intended. Leupold comments:

> There is a vagueness about the whole in point of time which invited men to trust God for whatever time He might be pleased to choose to bring it to fruition. Men had to be ready to settle down to a wait until it might please the sovereign Ruler to bring to pass what He here definitely had promised. . . . [And] by leaving open the question of just what woman the Saviour was to be born, God mocks the tempter, always leaving him in uncertainty which one would ultimately overthrow him, so that the devil had to live in continual dread of every woman's son that was born.[8]

If Genesis 3:15 be the *protoevangelium*, it would seem that 1 Timothy 2:15 should be Paul's inspired

---

7 Martin Luther remarked that "this text embraces and comprehends within itself everything noble and glorious that is to be found anywhere in the Scriptures."

8 H. C. Leupold, *Exposition of Genesis* (Grand Rapids, Michigan: Baker Book House, 1942), I, 168.

commentary upon it. In context he wrote that Eve, even though beguiled in that first transgression, "shall be saved in childbearing." The Greek reads "*the* child-bearing," as if pointing to a specific birth, *i.e.*, the incarnation of God in Christ. This is a marvelous truth: that just as woman was the instrument through whom sin came into the world, so was she the means whereby Messiah emerged. And this fact justifies our pressing the language of Genesis 3:15—"thy seed"—and finding an allusion to Galatians 4:4, "born of a woman." [9]

Genesis 3:15 and Galatians 4:4 represent the two poles between which the revelation of redemption was unfolded. The period of preparation from point of promise to "fulness of time" became necessary for at least three reasons: (1) to disclose to man the true nature of sin and depth of depravity to which he had digressed; (2) to exhibit to him his powerlessness to preserve or regain an adequate knowledge of God, or to effect by philosophy his own deliverance from sin; and (3) to teach him that forgiveness and restoration are possible only on the ground of a substitutionary sacrifice. History, strewn with the remains of humanistic endeavor, has demonstrated how imperfectly the world has learned these lessons; but a partial education in those principles, corresponding to man's capacities to receive

---

9 See W. Robertson Nicoll (ed.), *The Expositor's Greek Testament* (Grand Rapids, Michigan: Wm. B. Eerdmans Publishing Company, 1956), IV, 109-10.

It is interesting to note that *chattath*, "sin," in Genesis 4:7 may, in this place of its first occurrence, be rendered "sin-offering," so that here, as in the *protoevangelium*, God enlightens man as to alternative prospect. Some scholars suggest, however, that such an interpretation at this early stage in the progress of revelation presupposes too much prior instruction in sacrificial mode of worship.

them, was requisite to the introduction of the Saviour in person.[10]

The Substance of Revelation

Although the plan of salvation is one coherent whole, God employed numerous means to accomplish His objectives, and we are left in no doubt whatever as to the fact of divine and definite purpose. Paramount among those demonstrations of His grace in the progress of revelation are these singular institutions:[11]

(1) Theophanies. Those appearances of God to Moses (Exodus 33:11, 20-23), and even to the whole camp of Israel on occasion (Exodus 13:21, 19:16-18), confirmed and developed faith in a personal God. The same end was served by the various miracles wrought in Egypt (Exodus 7-12) and during the wilderness wanderings (Numbers 14ff.).

(2) Law. The specifications of certain divine demands were projected with the announced penalty which would follow failure to obey, arousing a conviction of guilt and a fear of the consequences of sin (Exodus 20-23).

(3) Sacrifice. Establishment of a system of sacrifice and a priesthood to administer it indicated a need of some procedure whereby to remove man's guilt, and also the provision of that method by God (Exodus 24-31; Leviticus 1-10, 16, 17, 21-23).

---

10 For a careful discussion of the principle of progressive revelation and the nature of biblical theology, see J. Barton Payne, *The Theology of the Older Testament* (Grand Rapids, Michigan: Zondervan Publishing House, 1962), pp. 17-9.

11 See *Ibid.*, pp. 257-84, and Thiessen, *op. cit.*, pp. 276-9. Cf. Patrick Fairbairn, *The Revelation of Law in Scripture* (Grand Rapids, Michigan: Zondervan Publishing House, 1957), *passim*.

(4) Prophecy. The prophets' annunciations of Christ were unusual for their clarity and force, pointing out the several aspects of His person and work having to bear upon divine deliverance.

(5) Typology. This facet of revelation was neither confined nor peculiar to any one period in the continuing experience of God's Old Testament people:

Persons in type of Christ included Adam (Genesis 1:26-31; Psalm 8:3-8; 1 Corinthians 15:21, 22, 45; Hebrews 2:8, 9), Melchizedek, the priest (Genesis 14:18-20; Hebrews 5:10, 6:20, 7:17), Joseph (Genesis 37:28; Matthew 2:14, 15), Moses, the prophet (Deuteronomy 18:15; Acts 3:22, 7:37), Joshua (Joshua 1:1, 2; Acts 7:45; Hebrews 2:10, 4: 8), David, the king (2 Samuel 7:13; Luke 1:32; Acts 13:22, 23), Solomon (1 Kings 10:7; Luke 11: 31), and Jonah (Jonah 1:17-2:10; Matthew 12:39-41).

Acts in type of Christ involve Isaac's sacrifice (Genesis 22:1-19; Hebrews 11:17-19) a n d the lifting up of the brazen serpent (Numbers 21:4-9; John 3:14, 15). Such was the purpose and providence of God in the Old Testament economy.

The prophets' annunciations deserve a further word. Basic predictions respecting the Messiah are numerous and well known.[12] But it is important here in illustration of the purpose of God to discern

---

12 *E.g.*, virgin birth (Isaiah 7:14; Matthew 1:23); birth at Bethlehem (Micah 5:2; Matthew 2:1); flight into Egypt (Hosea 11:1; Matthew 2:14, 15); character of His ministry (Isaiah 61:1, 2; Luke 4:16-21); circumstances of His death (Psalm 22; Isaiah 53; Matthew 26, 27); resurrection (Psalms 2, 110; Matthew 28; Acts 13:33; Romans 1:1-4); kingdom (Isaiah 9:6, 7; 11:1-9; Revelation 20:1-6).

a gradual specification and clarification of the revelation that had been committed first in the garden: in Genesis 3:15, the Redeemer would be a human being; in Genesis 9:6, a Semite; in Genesis 22: 18, 26:4, 28:14, of the lineage of Abraham, Isaac, and Jacob; in Genesis 49:10, of the tribe of Judah; in 2 Samuel 7:13, 16, of the house of David. Thus, from the seed of the woman to the family of David —from Eden to Bethlehem—God in His wisdom effected in history an incremental redemptive revelation culminating in His Son.

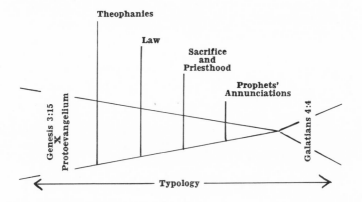

Jesus Christ, by whom the Father has spoken to us now in these last days, is the finality of revelation (Hebrews 1:1, 2). Warfield affirms that "in Jesus . . . all the lines of Messianic prediction converge; and they declare Him no less the Jehovah who was expected to come to save His people, than the Son of David or the Suffering Servant of God."[13]

13 Benjamin Breckinridge Warfield, *Biblical and Theological Studies.* ed. Samuel G. Craig (Philadelphia: The Presbyterian and Reformed Publishing Company, 1952), p. 103.

This is the fact—that God designed in Christ to reconcile the world unto Himself—allowing us to proceed with confidence to discussion of personal ramifications issuing from the eternal plan.

SUMMARY QUESTIONS

1. Define: soteriology, revelation, *protoevangelium,* Law, typology.
2. Distinguish between general and special revelation.
3. Discuss the progress of the revelation of redemption.
4. Cite some of the persons and acts in type of Christ.
5. Itemize a few of the specific prophecies regarding the person and work of Christ.

4

The Eternal Plan of God

The *ordo salutis,* or order of salvation, describes the process by which the work of salvation wrought in Christ is subjectively realized in the hearts and lives of sinners. It intends to present in their logical order, and also in their interrelationships, the several ministries of the Holy Spirit in applying the work of redemption. To delineate an *ordo salutis* is not to contradict the work of the Holy Spirit in commending the grace of God to the individual in a unitary process, but rather simply to stress the facts that various dispositions can be distinguished in the process, that the application of redemption proceeds in a definite and reasonable order, and that God does not impart the fulness of His salvation to the sinner in a single act.

The Bible is no more a system of theology than nature is a system of chemistry or mechanics. Just as the chemist or philosopher has to examine the facts of nature to ascertain the laws by which nature is determined, so the theologian collects, authenticates, arranges, and exhibits the truths of the Bible in their internal relationships to each other.

The Bible, furthermore, is the absolute and only factual repository for theological tenets, and by it all intuitive concerns, both intellectual and moral, must be measured.

The Ordo Salutis: An Overview

While the Bible does not explicitly furnish a complete order of salvation, it does offer us a sufficient basis for such an order. (The closest approximation to an *ordo salutis* in the Scriptures is Paul's statement in Romans 8:29, 30: "For whom he did foreknow, he also did predestinate to be conformed to the image of his Son, that he might be the firstborn among many brethren. Moreover whom he did predestinate, them he also called: and whom he called, them he also justified: and whom he justified, them he also glorified.") That basis is construed from the very full and rich enumeration of the operations of the Holy Spirit in applying the work of Christ to individual sinners and of the blessings of salvation imparted to them, and the constant indications of the relationships in which different ministries of the Holy Spirit in the work of redemption stand to each other.

Berkhof points out that construction of an *ordo salutis* is the fruit of the Reformation.[1] Because Protestantism represented a fundamental criticism and displacement of the Roman Catholic conception of faith, repentance, and good works, it was natural that the interests of the Reformers should center upon the origin and development of the new life in Christ. Divergent orders of salvation have arisen since John Calvin's first attempt at systematization,

---

1 L. Berkhof, *Systematic Theology* (Grand Rapids, Michigan: Wm. B. Eerdmans Publishing Company, 1941), p. 417.

but the essential elements in an evangelical rationale
are common to all of them. That order in the
economy of redemption preferred here is: foreknowledge, predestination, effectual calling, repentance, justification, regeneration, union with Christ
and adoption, sanctification, and glorification.[2]

The plan of God, of which the *ordo salutis* is the
subjective expression, is an eternal plan. Like the
decrees to create and to permit the fall, God's decrees to provide salvation and mediate that salvation
to all who believe are inscrutably immense in their
magnitude. By design, that plan extends into eternity past to the counsels of God Himself; by application, it projects into eternity future as the redeemed soul persists in conscious and cognitive activity.

The Lamb of God Elect

From eternity God ordained that His Son, having
been incarnated, should suffer vicariously for the sins
of the race, and that He should be resurrected from
the dead, ascend to intercede while in session with
the Father, and return to claim His own in the world.
Any intimation of divine afterthought as concerns
the condescension and humiliation of God's Son is
totally foreign to the Scriptures; nor do the so-called
"interim ethic" and "passover plot"—ideas to the effect that Jesus came initially to establish a political

---

2 This present study will not include discussion of the baptism with
the Holy Spirit. That doctrine itself would demand a detailed and ex-
clusive volume. Then, too, the experience, important as it is, does not
really find place within an *ordo salutis,* since it pertains not to salvation but to service. The baptism with the Holy Spirit is properly concerned with ecclesiology (the study of the church, *i.e.,* the Body of
Christ) rather than with soteriology, for it constitutes the power of the
Church, just as water baptism and holy communion are the sacraments
of the Church, and the second coming of Christ its blessed hope. (See
pp. 111-2.)

kingdom, but, frustrated by the pressure of contrary forces, He resigned Himself to a martyr's cross— have any justification in the Word.

The express understanding of Peter is that Jesus was "delivered by the determinate counsel and fore-knowledge of God" (Acts 2:23), that "God before had shewed by the mouth of all his prophets, that Christ should suffer" (Acts 3:18), that "against thy holy child Jesus, whom thou hast anointed, both Herod, and Pontius Pilate, with the Gentiles, and the people of Israel, were gathered together, For to do whatsoever thy hand and thy counsel determined before to be done" (Acts 4:27, 28), and that "Christ, as . . . a lamb without blemish and without spot: . . . verily was foreordained before the foundation of the world, but was manifest in these last times for you" (1 Peter 1:19, 20). Paul, furthermore, in a context concerning the unsearchable riches of Christ and the marvel of reconciliation, speaks of that "eternal purpose which he [the Father] pur-posed in Christ Jesus our Lord" (Ephesians 3:11). And John hails Him as "the Lamb slain from the foundation of the world" (Revelation 13:8).

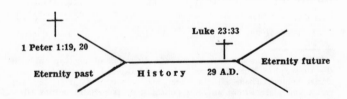

There was, then, a cross in eternity before one appeared in time. Calvary was the historical outworking of an event decreed before the foundation of the world. And nothing could have deterred God's plan, for what He decrees must necessarily come to pass. God does not make His plan or alter it as human history develops; He formulated it in eternity, constituting it static and unalterable. This inviolable nature of the divine decree issues not only from God's eternal purpose, but also from His most wise and holy counsel, from His freedom so to ordain, and from His concern for the ends of His own glory. That God's design should be of such certain character is a remarkable stimulus to personal faith, enhancing the believer's appreciation of His gracious and careful regard.

FOREKNOWLEDGE

Omniscience (all-knowledge) is an incommunicable attribute of God. That property is uniquely His, in no way whatever shared with the creature. The knowledge of God is perfect and totally comprehensive of all that is in nature and of all that occurs in human experience and human history. Whereas man's knowledge is limited, God's is infinite; and while man's knowledge is discursive, His is entire. Just as one may view the dimensions of a river only so far as his stance on the bank will permit, but may from some lofty height witness with one panoramic sweep its protracted expanse, so man discerns history in terms of disjointed segments of irregular duration, while God maintains an eternal vantage point. To Him who inhabits a realm where time, change, and sense perception are completely irrelevant, all things are perceived as transpiring in one whole, simultaneous present. (Cf. Isaiah 40, 57: 15; 2 Peter 3:8.) Thomas Aquinas, eminent Scholastic of the High Middle Ages, contended that God even knows all contingencies and alternatives as well as actualities.

Throughout the New Testament the foreknowledge (*prognosis*, "advance knowledge") of God respecting the mission of His Son is closely and conspicuously connected with His prevision of those who will be saved. If God were ignorant of the free acts of men, then His knowledge would be limited and in need of constant increase, which is altogether inconsistent with the true idea of His nature. But to say that God foreknows a thing is entirely different from saying that He foreordains it. To foreknow is to render a matter certain of fulfillment; to foreordain is to decree it as necessary.

God knew from eternity who among men would exercise free moral choice to embrace His Son in the forgiveness of sins, but that knowledge admits of neither overture nor constraint in violation of human freedom. The question as to why God should proceed with the creation of man when He foreknew the fall can be answered only in terms of the free extension of the social aspect of His nature, and the fact that He rejoiced in the certainty that some would choose to be saved through acceptance of His Son.

PREDESTINATION

Predestination is a fundamental doctrine of the Scriptures from which too many too often have retreated because of the intemperance of some theological camps. A remarkable and blessed teaching, it cannot be excised from the *ordo salutis* without impairing the whole.

Otherwise called foreordination or election, predestination (from *prooridzo,* "to determine the boundaries of beforehand") refers to the sovereign and free act of God's grace whereby from eternity He chose in Christ Jesus for Himself and for salvation all those who He foreknew would respond positively to His overtures of love. It is *sovereign* and *free* because God was under no necessity or obligation to elect anyone; it is of *grace,* and therefore truly unconditional, in the sense that it does not rest upon human deserts; it is *in Christ* in that it is based solely upon His merits.

Since predestination proceeds from foreknowledge (Romans 8:29; 1 Peter 1:1, 2), and the sovereign decisions of God are not arbitrarily determined, sovereignty and free will become compatible. God is sovereign in His design and initiation of redemption, decreeing completely without necessity; man remains free and fully responsible for intelligent and volitional option.

Ephesians 1:4, 5 is a primary source for the doctrine of predestination: "According as he hath chosen us in him before the foundation of the world, that we should be holy and without blame before him in love: Having predestinated us unto the adoption of children by Jesus Christ to himself, according to the good pleasure of his will." This prodigious Pauline insight delineates five urgently significant facets of the election of God:

(1) Its source is placed in God's love;

(2) Its meritorious cause is the mediation of the Lord Jesus Christ;

(3) Its result is adoption into the family of God;

(4) It is in itself the expression of "the good pleasure of his will," on which will all ultimately depends; and

(5) Its final purpose is to display God's glory in the gift of His grace.[3]

Paul proceeds further to call us the "heritage" of Christ (American Standard Version), because we have been "predestinated according to the purpose of him who worketh all things after the counsel of his own will" (Ephesians 1:11). And in 2 Thessalonians 2:13 he affirms with clarity that "God hath from the beginning chosen . . . [us] to salvation through sanctification of the Spirit and belief of the truth."

EFFECTUAL CALLING

The grace of God is commended and magnified, not only in the provision of salvation, but also in its being offered to the undeserving. Effectual calling (or vocation) is that gracious appeal by which God invites men to accept by faith His salvation effected in Christ. There is no biblical justification for distinguishing between a general or external call to all men and a special, efficacious call to the elect. Sal-

---

3 See Donald N. Bowdle (ed.), *Ellicott's Bible Commentary* (Grand Rapids, Michigan: Zondervan Publishing House, 1971), p. 1031; and Henry C. Thiessen, *Introductory Lectures in Systematic Theology* (Grand Rapids, Michigan: Wm. B. Eerdmans Publishing Company, 1949), pp. 156-7, 344-5.

vation is freely offered to all; "whosoever will" may come (Revelation 22:17). God's offer of salvation is universal in range, for He desires to save all men and to extend the same enabling grace to those who choose Him.

God's call goes forth in many different ways: sermon, hymn, literature, providential dealings. All such means are but efficient employment of the Holy Spirit in His application of the Word, which to believe is life eternal.

SUMMARY QUESTIONS

1. Define: *ordo salutis,* omniscience, foreknowledge, predestination, effectual calling.
2. What is meant by the expression "eternal plan of God"?
3. Relate the sovereignty of God to the free will of man.
4. By what means does God "call" the sinner?
5. Why is the baptism with the Holy Spirit not a part of the order of salvation?

PART TWO

REDEMPTION APPLIED

The Scriptures teach us to recognize a certain economy in the work of redemption, warranting our speaking of the Father in its design, of the Son in its execution, and of the Holy Spirit in its application. As pertains to the latter, the Scriptures assert that He originates, maintains, develops, and guides the new life that is born from above, is nourished from above, and will be perfected above—a life which, as Berkhof notes, is "heavenly in principle, though lived on earth."[1] By His special operation the Holy Spirit overcomes the power of sin, renews man in the image of God, and enables him to offer that spiritual obedience rendering him the salt of the earth, the light of the world, and a spiritual leaven in every dimension of life.

An attribute of God—one of the divine perfections —and a designation for the objective provision which God made in Christ for the salvation of sinners, *charis,* "grace," extends beyond the unmerited favor of God in the subjective application of the work of redemption, to embrace all the spiritual blessings wrought by the Holy Spirit for the advantage of believers.

Part Two of this study discusses the vital and expulsive nature of this new affection.

---

1 L. Berkhof, *Systematic Theology* (Grand Rapids, Michigan: Wm. B. Eerdmans Publishing Company, 1941), p. 426.

5

Repentance and Justification

God always takes the initiative in matters relating to salvation. Not only did He come to mankind generally in the events of Incarnation and Calvary, but He encounters men individually through the Holy Spirit's asserting the redemptive claims of Jesus Christ. Repentance constitutes the sinner's positive response to this calling of God; and thus effectually called, the sinner is justified by an act of divine reciprocity.

REPENTANCE

Repentance was a central message of the Old Testament prophets (Isaiah 55:7; Jeremiah 8:6; Ezekiel 14:6, 18:30), of John the Baptist (Matthew 3:2), of Jesus (Mark 1:15; Luke 13:3, 5), and of the Twelve (Mark 6:12). It was a deliberate, integral, and clearly identified inclusion of the *kerygma,* or pattern of apostolic preaching, as evidenced by Peter on the Day of Pentecost (Acts 2:38) and by Paul (Acts 17:30, 20:21, 26:20). This is an experience, furthermore, in which heaven is supremely interested (Luke 15:7, 10, 24:46, 47). Thiessen calls it "the fundamental of fundamentals . . . because it is an absolute condition to salvation. . . ."[1]

The Psychology of Repentance

"Repentance" and "conversion" are used in close relationship, although the former word is better related to forsaking one's sins (negative), and the latter to turning toward God (positive). They refer to what is basically an act of faith, whereby there is effected a change of mind, a change of course, and a change of conduct. The Old Testament uses two particular Hebrew verbs to convey this idea. One is *nacham*, serving to express a deep feeling, either of sorrow or relief, accompanied by an alteration of plan and action. The other is *shuv*, which designates a turning around, of frequent use in the prophets in summoning Israel to return to Him from whom sin had separated them.[2]

Three words, principally, are employed in the New Testament to identify this experience. *Metanoia* is the most common and fundamental. Trench points out that in the classics its verb cognate *metanoeo* means: (1) to know after, afterknowledge; (2) to change the mind as the result of this after-knowledge; (3) to regret the course pursued, in consequence of this change of mind; and, (4) to change conduct for the future, issuing

---

1 Henry C. Thiessen, *Introductory Lectures in Systematic Theology* (Grand Rapids, Michigan: Wm. B. Eerdmans Publishing Company, 1949), p. 353. Cf. F. F. Bruce, *The Book of Acts* (in *The New International Commentary on the New Testament;* Grand Rapids, Michigan: Wm. B. Eerdmans Publishing Company, 1956), pp. 50, 69.

2 See Robert B. Girdlestone, *Synonyms of the Old Testament* (Grand Rapids, Michigan: Wm. B. Eerdmans Publishing Company, 1897), pp. 87-93.

from all the preceding. In the New Testament, however, its meaning is deepened, denoting primarily a change of mind, taking a wiser view of the past, including regret for the ill then done and leading to a change of life for the better. *Epistrophe* and *metameleia,* nouns used but infrequently in the New Testament, stress almost completely the act of turning, *i.e.,* the establishing of a new relationship in which the active life is made to move in another direction.[3]

These words indicate that repentance (or conversion) is an experience admitting three important aspects—*intellectual, volitional,* and *emotional:*

The intellectual dimension to repentance involves a change of view with regard to sin, to God, and to self: sin comes to be recognized as personal guilt; God, as One justly demanding righteousness; self, as helpless and defiled (cf. Job 42:56; Psalm 51:3, 7). This aspect of repentance represents an intellectual encounter with the issues of the gospel, the fruit of which is a rational decision based squarely upon a discernment of those laws of spiritual life.

The volitional element involves a change of disposition, in that one willfully turns away from self and toward God (cf. Acts 8:22). Here is a conscious aversion to the former way of life, comprised of ignorance, error, and folly, and a deliberate choice whereby a new pursuit is engaged.

The emotional facet of repentance concerns the sorrow for sin and desire for pardon that accrue

---

3 See Richard C. Trench, *Synonyms of the New Testament* (Grand Rapids, Michigan: Wm. B. Eerdmans Publishing Company, 1958), pp. 255-6.

from prior intelligent decision and willful purpose (cf. 2 Corinthians 7:10).

It is important that this order in repentance—intellectual, volitional, and emotional—be maintained, for the joy of sins forgiven cannot fully be experienced until an elementary understanding of the gospel is reached and a positive commitment made to it.

Alan Richardson suggests that *metanoia* "involves a whole reorientation of the personality."[4] Perhaps the parable of the prodigal son in Luke 15 illustrates this best in the several aspects of response to the calling of God. Rebellious to the point of having "spent all," the young adventurer identified with a menial task completely incommensurate with his background and capabilities. But "he came to himself" (intellectual, or change of mind, verse 17), realizing his miserable plight apart from privilege; he determined that "I will arise and go to my father" (volitional, or change of course, verse 18); he purposed to confess that "I have sinned" (emotional, or change of conduct, verse 18). Is not this the experience of "everyman"?

The Agency of Faith

Faith is crucial to an experience of repentance. The Bible distinguishes several different kinds of faith: *e.g.*, faith as a grace whereby to live the practical Christian life (Romans 12:3); faith as a gift of the Holy Spirit (1 Corinthians 12:9); *the* faith, being the sum total of Christian doctrine as committed in the Scriptures (1 Timothy 4:1, 6:10;

---

4 Alan Richardson (ed.), *A Theological Wordbook of the Bible* (New York: The Macmillan Company, 1950), p. 192.

Jude 3). But the faith to which reference here is made is "saving faith," as Ephesians 2:8, 9 seems to project: "For by grace are ye saved through faith; and that not of yourselves: it is the gift of God: Not of works, lest any man should boast." Cognate to *pisteuo* ("to believe"), faith *(pistis)* in this sense is an action word, connoting the state of absolute transference of trust from oneself to another—a complete self-surrender to God.[5]

Ephesians 2:8, 9 is constructed in such a way in the Greek as to assure us that not only grace, but neither grace *nor* faith, is inherently man's, rendering the whole of salvation as of God. Salvation "is not the result of a natural evolution of character, and yet more it is not the result of self-originated and self-supported effort."[6] Thus precluding all merit and human effort,—for man is naturally devoid of "ability Godward,"—the Apostle Paul here concedes only the active exercise of free moral agency in relation to that faith of Jesus Christ (cf. Galatians 2:20). Saving faith is offered by the Holy Spirit along with His convicting of sin in presentation of the issues of the gospel. By intelligent and willful option the sinner either allows or disallows that faith to operate effectually.

The hymn has said it well:

---

5 L. Berkhof, *Systematic Theology* (Grand Rapids, Michigan: Wm. B. Eerdmans Publishing Company, 1941), pp. 494-5, 503; cf. Joseph Henry Thayer, *A Greek-English Lexicon of the New Testament* (fourth edition; Edinburgh: T & T Clark, 1901), pp. 511-4.

6 Brooke Foss Westcott, *Epistle to the Ephesians* (London: Macmillan and Co., Limited, 1906), p. 32. Cf. A. T. Robertson, *A Grammar of the Greek New Testament in the Light of Historical Research.* (Nashville: Broadman Press, 1934), p. 1182.

"I know not how the Spirit moves,
Convincing men of sin;
Revealing Jesus through the Word,
Creating faith in Him."[7]

Repentance is, then, in this sense an act of the will in positive response to the calling of the Holy Spirit and by His own enablement. Once a conversion has ensued, the believer positions himself as liable for the multiple and copious blessings in his life. As repentance and conversion constitute man's response to the initiative which God has taken in His free and sovereign overtures of grace, so now the remaining conditions of the *ordo salutis* identify God's further working in his behalf.

It would be well at this juncture to relate those several ministries of the Holy Spirit both to each other and to the various aspects of sin in man's existence to which they are designed to answer:

We remember in retrospect that sin is a nature, rendering man depraved; an estate, certifying his inability consistently to please God; and an act, producing in him feelings of guilt for inevitable violations of divine law.

We note in prospect that justification is an objective act ministering to the guilt for deeds of sin committed; regeneration is a subjective act ministering to the estate of inability because of the moral erosion effected by sin; sanctification is both subjective act and process ministering to the nature or cause of sin in the life. Justification concerns what God has done *for* us, while regeneration and sanctification pertain to what He does *in* us.

---

7 Daniel W. Whittle and James McGranahan, "I Know Whom I Have Believed," stanza 3.

SIN	*MAN*	*MINISTRY*
nature	depravity	sanctification
estate	inability	regeneration
act	guilt	justification

JUSTIFICATION

Although some of the earliest and most articulate Church Fathers spoke of justification by faith, the doctrine did not find its explicit expression until the Reformation. The great material principle of that movement, justification was emphasized as a free act of God issuing from that faith which receives Christ and rests in Him alone for salvation. The Reformers rejected any teaching of a progressive justification, contending, unlike the terms of their Roman Catholic antecedents, that it was instantaneous and complete, depending upon no further satisfaction for sin.

The Meaning and Method of Justification

The Hebrew term for "to justify" is *tsadak,* meaning, more fully, "to declare judicially that one's state is in harmony with the demands of the law" (Exodus 23:7; Isaiah 5:23). Also forensic or legal in nature, the Greek *dikaioo,* used in the classical dialect for a wagon or a horse "fit" for its intended purpose, signifies in the New Testament "to effect an objective relation, the state of righteousness by a judicial sentence" (Romans 5:1, 9, 8:33, 34).[8]

---

8 Berkhof, *op. cit.,* pp. 510-1. Cf. Francis Brown, S. R. Driver, and Charles A. Briggs, *A Hebrew and English Lexicon of the Old Testament* (Oxford: Oxford University Press, 1907), pp. 841-3; and William F. Arndt and F. Wilbur Gingrich, *A Greek-English Lexicon of the New Testament and Other Early Christian Literature* (Chicago: University of Chicago Press, 1957), pp. 194-7.

These verbs prompted John Calvin to interpret justification as "the acceptance with which God receives us into his favor as if we were righteous"; "and . . . this justification," he continued, "consists in the forgiveness of sins and the imputation of the righteousness of Christ."[9] One of the most adequate confessional statements is that "justification is an act of God's free grace, wherein he pardoneth all our sins, and accepteth us as righteous in his sight, only for the righteousness of Christ imputed to us, and received by faith alone."[10]

As to the method of justification, the Scriptures teach that:

(1) It is *not* by the works of the law (Romans 3:20, "Therefore by the deeds of the law there shall no flesh be justified in his sight: for by the law is the knowledge of sin");

(2) It is by the grace of God (Romans 3:24, "Being justified freely by his grace through the redemption that is in Christ Jesus"; Titus 3:7, "That being justified by his grace, we should be made heirs according to the hope of eternal life");

(3) It is by the blood of Christ (Romans 5:9, "Much more then, being now justified by his blood, we shall be saved from wrath through him"); and,

(4) It is by faith (Galatians 2:16, "Knowing that a man is not justified by the works of the law, but by the faith of Jesus Christ").

On these certain grounds it may confidently be

---

9 John Calvin, *Institutes of the Christian Religion*, trans. Henry Beveridge (Grand Rapids, Michigan: Wm. B. Eerdmans Publishing Company, 1962), II, 37-8.
10 Westminster Shorter Catechism, Article 33.

affirmed that "man is either fully justified, or he is not justified at all."[11]

The Provisions of Justification

"And whom he called, them he also justified" (Romans 8:30). So reads an integral part of the Pauline *ordo salutis*. But just what are the benefits of this experience of grace? To be justified is to share in three particular provisions of God in Christ:

First is the *forgiveness of sins,* which is tantamount to acquittal of guilt and remission of penalty. All sin is an affront to the holiness of God and must be punished. Christ bore the punishment of our sins in His own body on the tree (Isaiah 53:5, 6; 1 Peter 2:24). Since He has borne man's penalty for sin, God now remits it in the case of him who believes on Christ. By His action God has a just ground whereby to deal further with the individual, remaining both "just, and the justifier of him which believeth in Jesus" (Romans 3:26).

A second provision of justification is *restoration to favor with God,* so that the believer partakes of all the filial rights incident to his change in status. "Therefore being justified by faith," Paul wrote, "we have peace with God through our Lord Jesus Christ" (Romans 5:1). "Peace" to which reference here is made is the cessation of hostilities between God and man, the forging of that reconciliation requisite to an efficient claiming of the privileges of sonship.[12]

---

11 Berkhof, *op. cit.,* p. 513.
12 See William Sanday and Arthur C. Headlam, The *Epistle to the Romans* (eleventh edition; in *The International Critical Commentary,* ed. Charles A. Briggs, S. R. Driver, and Alfred Plummer. New York: Charles Scribner's Sons, 1906), pp. 119-21.

The third benefit of justification is the *imputation of the righteousness of Christ*. Not only must sins be pardoned, but positive righteousness must be put on one's account before he can experience fellowship. Paul extols this wonderful truth in 2 Corinthians 5:21: "Him [Christ] who knew no sin he [the Father] made to be sin on our behalf; that we might become the righteousness of God in him" (American Standard Version).

In this important Corinthian passage the Apostle states that Christ was made sin in our behalf, because the idea of substitution is involved in the very nature of the transaction. Charles Hodge is of the opinion that

> there is probably no passage in the Scriptures in which the doctrine of justification is more concisely or clearly stated than in this. Our sins were imputed to Christ, and his righteousness is imputed to us. . . . Our sins were the judicial ground of the sufferings of Christ, so that they were a satisfaction of justice; and his righteousness is the judicial ground of our acceptance with God, so that our pardon is an act of justice. It is a justification; or, a declaration that justice is satisfied. We are set free by no mere act of sovereignty, but by the judicial decision of the infinitely just. As we, considered in ourselves, are just as undeserving and hell-deserving as ever, this justification is to us an act of infinite grace. The special consideration, therefore, by which the apostle enforces the exhortation, "Be ye reconciled to God" [verse 20], is that God can be just in the justification of sinners. There is nothing in the perfection of his character, nothing in the immutability of his law, nothing in the interests of his moral government, that stands in the way of our pardon. A full, complete, infinitely meritorious satisfaction has been made for our sins,

and therefore we may come to God with the assurance of being accepted.[13]

Luther remarked, and well so, pertaining both to justification effected and regeneration anticipated, that "he who denies certainty of salvation rejects faith."[14]

SUMMARY QUESTIONS

1. Define: repentance, *kerygma*, justification, faith, remission.

2. Distinguish between repentance and conversion.

3. What are the three important aspects of repentance?

4. What do the Scriptures teach about the method of justification?

5. What are the provisions of justification?

---

13 Charles Hodge, *An Exposition of the Second Epistle to the Corinthians* (Grand Rapids, Michigan: Wm. B. Eerdmans Publishing Company, n.d.), pp. 150-1.

14 Quoted in Erich Sauer, *The Triumph of the Crucified; A Study of Historical Revelation in the New Testament*, trans. G. H. Lang (Grand Rapids, Michigan: Wm. B. Eerdmans Publishing Company, 1955), p. 95.

6

Regeneration, and Union With Christ and Adoption

God's blessings in salvation extend beyond the external ground and declarative assignment of merit, to include an intimate and vital relationship between Himself and those who have been effectually called. Justification and regeneration are concomitant experiences. Whereas the former is *objective* and addresses the guilt for acts of sin committed, the latter is *subjective*, constituting divine compensation for elemental inability in spiritual pursuit.

It may be posited another way: Justification is a matter of *imputation,* what God does *for* the believer; regeneration has to do with *impartation,* what He does *in* the believer. The practical issue of these closely associated acts of God is a new and marvelous status in the economy of grace.

REGENERATION

The rationale of regeneration proceeds in an orderly fashion from the basic scriptural premise of man's inherent impotence in spiritual things. Since the fall, men of every age, every nation, and every condition are represented as spiritually dead, destitute of the life of God. Their understanding is darkened and their sensibilities dulled; and thus alienated from God, they are wholly and utterly unable to deliver themselves from that estate of corruption and misery.

Regeneration may be defined simply as the communication of divine life to the soul (1 John 5:11, 12), as the impartation of a new nature (2 Peter 1:4), and as the production of a new creation (2 Corinthians 5:17). It is a creative work of God in which man is entirely passive, and in which there is no place for human cooperation. The Holy Spirit is the efficient causal agent of regeneration, the only recourse whereby the sinner, spiritually dead, may be restored to life. An act of God whereby the principle of new life is implanted in the soul, and the governing disposition of the soul made holy, regeneration is mediated by the Word of God (James 1:18; 1 Peter 1:23). "It is the same Word that is heard in the external call, and that is made effective in the heart in the internal calling. Through the powerful application of the Holy Spirit the external call passes right into the internal."[1]

Palingenesia, "regeneration" or "new birth," is found in the Greek New Testament only in Matthew 19:28 and Titus 3:5, and only in the latter passage is this noun used in reference to the beginning of the new life in the individual Christian. More frequently used in this regard are the verbs *gennao* (or *anagennao*), "to beget, to beget again, to give birth,"

---

1 L. Berkhof, *Systematic Theology* (Grand Rapids, Michigan: Wm. B. Eerdmans Publishing Company, 1941), p. 469.

and *zoopoieo* (or *suzoopoieo*), "to quicken, to make alive with."[2]

These verbs are employed characteristically in three paramount passages teaching regeneration—the former in John 3:3-8, and the latter in Romans 8:1-11 and Ephesians 2:1-10. These, together with certain supplementary references that may be brought to bear, project the doctrine in terms of a new principle, a new pursuit, and a new perspective.

A New Principle

A new principle is imparted in remedial measure for the natural condition of man, described by Paul as dead in trespasses and sins, depraved, and alienated from the life of God (Romans 8:6; Ephesians 2:1, 5). This principle of new life is produced by the active agency of the Holy Spirit, and that through what is commonly called the new birth (John 3:3-8). Just as in the natural sphere a child cannot be born except through the depositing of seed through union, so in the spiritual a child of God cannot be born except by the implanting of the Word by the Holy Spirit Himself (1 John 3:9, 1 Peter 1:23).[3] The Christian, then, is possessor of a gift in which he could not before have delight. Peter says that we have been made partakers of the divine nature (2 Peter 1:4).

Romans 8:11 is a key consideration in the matter of the divine impartation of new life: "But if the Spirit of him that raised up Jesus from the dead

---

2 See William F. Arndt and F. Wilbur Gingrich, *A Greek-English Lexicon of the New Testament and Other Early Christian Literature* (Chicago: University of Chicago Press, 1957), pp. 51, 154-5, 342, 783.

3 W. Robertson Nicoll (ed.), *The Expositor's Greek Testament* (Grand Rapids, Michigan: Wm. B. Eerdmans Publishing Company, 1956), V, 185.

dwell in you, he that raised up Christ from the dead shall also quicken your mortal bodies by his Spirit that dwelleth in you." As in Ephesians 2:5 and Colossians 2:13, "quicken" ("to make alive" and "to give life" according to the American Standard Version) is the compound Greek verb *zoopoieo*. Paul alludes here both to the Holy Spirit's raising the soul spiritually dead to newness of life, and to His divine action upon the mortal frame in that future event of bodily resurrection. One of the most blessed thoughts in all of God's Word is found here: the same Holy Spirit who was operative in raising Jesus from the dead physically on that first Easter morning has also touched us in our resurrection to spiritual life. Resurrection, then, is not a future concept only, but every Christian has, by virtue of his regeneration, already experienced resurrection power.

It is urgent to maintain here that every Christian possesses the Holy Spirit in regenerating measure. "Now if any man have not the Spirit of Christ," Paul announces, "he is none of his" (Romans 8:9; see also 1 Corinthians 6:19). This is not to assert that every Christian has been baptized with the Holy Spirit. *Indwelling* and *infilling* are two completely different experiences. (See John 7:37-39.) Without the former, one cannot be a child of God at all; without the latter, he cannot be fully effective in His service.[4]

Realization of this indwelling of the Spirit brings great blessing. "Every other bond of union with Christ is of no avail without this. . . . Unless we are partakers of that vital union which arises from the

---

4 See note on page 61.

indwelling of the Holy Ghost, we are his only in name."[5] And so the spiritual image of God in man, marred by the fall, is renewed by the direct agency of the Holy Spirit Himself (see Ephesians 4:24; Colossians 3:10).

A New Pursuit

A new pursuit commensurate with the new life imparted to the believer is everywhere admonished in the Scriptures. Through the power of the indwelling Spirit, the child of God seeks the way pleasing to Him rather than the carnal walk of a previous time. The Holy Spirit produces nine graces which Paul designates in Galatians 5:22, 23 as the fruit of the Spirit. Such marks of character as imposed here are totally foreign to natural man and can be realized only through renewal by the Holy Spirit.

According to Lightfoot,[6] the ninefold fruit of the Spirit admits division into three broad areas:

(1) The first triad concerns Christian habits of mind in their more general aspect, comprising love, the foundation; joy, the superstructure; and peace, the crown of all.

(2) The second triad pertains to those special qualities affecting one's dealings with his neighbor, such as longsuffering, a patient endurance under injuries inflicted by others; gentleness, a kindly dis-

---

5 Charles Hodge, *Commentary on the Epistle to the Romans* (Grand Rapids, Michigan: Wm. B. Eerdmans Publishing Company, n.d.), p. 257.
6 J. B. Lightfoot, *The Epistle of St. Paul to the Galatians* (second edition; Grand Rapids, Michigan: Zondervan Publishing House, 1957), pp. 212-3. Cf. Bennie S. Triplett, *A Contemporary Study of the Holy Spirit* (Cleveland, Tennessee: Pathway Press, 1970), pp. 89-110.

position toward one's fellowman; and goodness or beneficence, an energetic principle.

(3) The third triad includes those principles, general in character like the first, which guide the exhibition of Christian conduct, namely faith, or trustworthiness and honesty in one's treatment of others; meekness, the proper attitude toward self; and temperance, or self-control in all matters.

This roster of virtues is designed to give immediate contrast to the catalog of sins issuing from the carnal nature. In these few well-chosen words the Apostle cites the enormous gulf in nature and conduct separating the unregenerate from the regenerate. J. B. Phillips renders this contrast in an interesting way:

> The activities of the lower nature are obvious. Here is a list: sexual immorality, impurity of mind, sensuality, worship of false gods, witchcraft, hatred, quarreling, jealousy, bad temper, rivalry, factions, party spirit, envy, drunkenness, orgies, and things like that. I solemnly assure you, as I did before, that those who indulge in such things will never inherit God's kingdom. The Spirit, however, produces in human life fruits such as these: love, joy, peace, patience, kindness, generosity, fidelity, tolerance and self-control—and no law exists against any of them. (Galatians 5:19-23)

Law exists for the purpose of restraint, but in the works of the Spirit there is nothing to restrain. These graces are meant to abound in the life to the glory of God. In His Son the affections and lusts of the flesh have been crucified. By the power of the Holy Spirit one is enabled to pursue the nobler course, demonstrating those attitudes and actions which are contrary to the disposition of the world.

No thought carries with it more solemn implications than that of the indwelling of the Holy Spirit. His action has been posited both as immediate and iterative. It is immediate in that regeneration, a restoration to life which issues in reinstatement to divine favor, occupies but one blessed moment; it is iterative because this implanted seed of God yields in abundant and abiding proportions the fruit of godliness.

A New Perspective

A new perspective is gained when we ask some basic questions: *e.g.;* What is the more pragmatic composition of this fundamental Christian tenet? and, How much emphasis may properly be brought to bear upon the matter of cultivating the fruit of the Spirit? Note, in response, these three very important considerations:

(1) All Christians are to be like this. Such is not merely the description of some exceptional Christian, but it is God's description of every single Christian;

(2) Not only are these characteristics designed for all Christians, but all Christians are meant to manifest all of them; and,

(3) None of these virtues refers to what we may call a natural tendency. Each is wholly a disposition which is produced by grace alone and the operation of the Holy Spirit within the believer.

With regard to these graces, therefore, it is imperative to remember that we are not told, "Live like this and you will *become* Christian"; but, rather, we are challenged, "Live like this because you *are* Christian."

UNION WITH CHRIST AND ADOPTION

The justified and regenerated individual is brought, by virtue of those very acts of grace, into a vital union with Christ. It follows from that prior federal or representative union whereby He, as the Second Adam (1 Corinthians 15:22), assumed those broken obligations which Adam failed to discharge, and fulfilled them all in behalf of mankind. But even so, this new relationship pursuant upon forgiveness and new birth is effected on the most personal and intimate terms.

Participation in Christ

Two particular approaches are taken in the Scriptures toward identifying the nature of this union between Christ and the believer:

One is the frequent analogies drawn from earthly relationships. These include the union between a building and its foundation (Ephesians 2:20-22; Colossians 2:7; 1 Peter 2:4, 5); the union between husband and wife (Romans 7:4; Ephesians 5:31, 32; Revelation 19:7-9); the union between the vine and its branches (John 15:5; Romans 6:5); and the union between the head and the body (1 Corinthians 6:15, 19, 12:12; Ephesians 1:22, 23, 4:15, 16).

Another approach is the many direct statements of this fact of union: Jesus spoke of believers as being "in" Him (John 14:20); Paul refers repeatedly to believers' being "in Christ" (Romans 6:11, 8:1; 2 Corinthians 5:17; Ephesians 1:4, 2:13; Colossians 2:8-15); Father, Son and Holy Spirit are said to indwell believers (John 14:20, 23; Romans 8:9-11; Galatians 2:20; Colossians 1:27); and believers are represented as partaking of Christ (John 6:53, 56,

57; 1 Corinthians 10:16, 17), as receiving the divine nature (2 Peter 1:4), and as being one spirit with the Lord (1 Corinthians 6:17).

From these scriptural observations it is clear that this union is *not* the mystical kind of the pantheist, nor the inclusive kind of the universalist, nor the sympathetic kind of friends, nor the abstract kind of the philosopher, nor the physical or material kind of the sacramentarian. What *is* this union, then? We may assert positively that it is:

(1) a spiritual union, of which the Holy Spirit Himself is the Author;

(2) a vital union, absolutely indispensable for spiritual nourishment and persevering grace;

(3) a complete union, needing no complement of any kind in deference to deficiency;

(4) an inscrutible union, which must forever remain in the realm of mystery; and,

(5) a secure union, in that the power of eternal life is presently operative within us to the praise and honor of Jesus Christ.[7]

Sonship With the Father

Adoption is not a doctrine separate from union with Christ, but rather it's a natural and necessary issue. Referring to the new status of the believer-in-

---

7 Henry C. Thiessen, *Introductory Lectures in Systematic Theology* (Grand Rapids, Michigan: Wm. B. Eerdmans Publishing Company, 1949), pp. 370-2.

Because of the volume of contrary persuasion, it should be pointed out here that a *secure* union (John 10:28-30; Romans 8:38, 39) does not mean an *inviolable* one. As it is possible for man to resist the prevenient grace of God in His offer of salvation, so he may, once saved, exercise his free will to the forfeiture of eternal life. See pp. 64-7, 72-4, 102-3.

Christ, adoption is a purely Pauline teaching, the Greek noun *huiothesia* appearing in the New Testament only in Paul's letters (Romans 8:15, 23, 9:4; Galatians 4:5; Ephesians 1:5). *Huiothesia* means, literally, "placing as a son," and may be defined as an act of God's grace whereby one already a child is, through redemption from the law, placed in the position of an adult son.

The Apostle conceives of man outside Christ as morally an alien and a stranger from God, and the change wrought by faith in Christ as making him morally a son and conscious of his sonship. Once a son, the regenerated one becomes so intimately united with Christ that His filial spirit enters into him and takes possession of his consciousness, so that he knows and greets the Father as Christ does (Mark 14:36).[8]

Adoption admits a threefold time relationship in its effects to the believer:

(1) It *was* an act in the counsel of God in eternity past (Ephesians 1:5);

(2) It *is* an actual, personal experience at the moment of accepting Christ as Saviour (Galatians 3:26); and,

(3) It *will be* consummated, *i.e.,* realized in its full dimension as sonship, at the second coming of Christ (Romans 8:23).

Presently led by the Holy Spirit in terms of mental and moral affections (Romans 8:14; Galatians 5:

---

8 See James Orr, *et. al.* (eds.), *The International Standard Bible Encyclopedia* (Grand Rapids, Michigan: Wm. B. Eerdmans Publishing Company, 1939), I, 58-60.

18), the adopted son of God learns an incremental conformity to the image of God's Son (Romans 8: 29), allowing even further enlargement upon the blessings of grace.

SUMMARY QUESTIONS

1. Define: regeneration, temperance, union, adoption, conformity.
2. Distinguish between justification and regeneration.
3. Distinguish between the indwelling and the infilling of the Holy Spirit.
4. Identify the fruit of the Spirit.
5. Discuss the nature of the believer's union with Christ.

7

Sanctification and Glorification

The redemptive provisions heretofore delineated in the *ordo salutis* have been *constructive* in design. Inherent in sanctification, however, is a *destructive* element, nevertheless intended to complement and enhance the progress of grace in the Christian life. Whereas justification deals with sin as an act (man's guilt), and regeneration concerns sin as an estate (man's inability), sanctification ministers to sin as a nature (man's depravity).

Calvin, unlike Luther and certain other Reformers, clearly distinguished between regeneration and sanctification, but it remained for the Wesleyan revivalism of the eighteenth century to commend in a really urgent manner the prospects of this important tenet of the Christian faith.

Glorification ensues in God's own time as the terminative experience of grace, tantamount to the believer's ultimate transformation and transfer into that eternity from whence his calling originated.

SANCTIFICATION

The Church of God was a holiness church before it became a pentecostal church. Holiness is both the prerequisite and the continuing condition of the Spirit-filled life. The experience and practice of holiness remains a basic tenet of our denomination's faith. Articles 6 and 7 of the Church of God Declaration of Faith affirm that we believe "in sanctification subsequent to the new birth, through faith in the blood of Christ; through the Word, and by the Holy Ghost" and "holiness to be God's standard of living for His people."

Sanctification is vitally related to those preceding operations in the *ordo salutis*. In sanctification the new nature of the believer is sustained and his status in grace confirmed.

Linguistic Observations

Any responsible treatment of the doctrine of sanctification properly begins with some consideration of biblical terminology.[1] Those words most crucial to the study are the verbs *kadash* and *hagiadzo*, and their derived forms in the Hebrew and Greek languages respectively. Both sources mean, basically, "to separate" and "to cleanse." The Hebrew root *kdsh* in its various and versatile in-

---

1 See Francis Brown, S. R. Driver, and Charles A. Briggs, *A Hebrew and English Lexicon of the Old Testament* (Oxford: Oxford University Press, 1907), pp. 871-4; Robert B. Girdlestone, *Synonyms of the Old Testament* (Grand Rapids, Michigan: Wm. B. Eerdmans Publishing Company, 1897), pp. 175-82; Gerhard Kittel (ed.), *Theological Dictionary of the New Testament*, trans. Geoffrey W. Bromiley (Grand Rapids, Michigan: Wm. B. Eerdmans Publishing Company, 1964-), I, 88-115; Alan Richardson (ed.), *A Theological Wordbook of the Bible* (New York: The Macmillan Company, 1950), pp. 216-9; and Richard C. Trench, *Synonyms of the New Testament* (Grand Rapids, Michigan: Wm. B. Eerdmans Publishing Company, 1958), pp. 74-7, 331-4.

flections is applied in the Old Testament to places (Jerusalem, Nehemiah 11:1; the temple, 1 Kings 9:3), to times (the Sabbath, Exodus 20:8, 11; the fiftieth year, Leviticus 25:10), and to persons (the firstborn, Exodus 13:2; the priests, Exodus 28:41).

In every case the point involved is relation or contact with God. Perhaps the English word "sacred" represents the idea better than "holy." The terms "sanctification" and "holiness" are used so frequently to indicate moral and spiritual qualities that they hardly ever convey the concepts of *position* or *relationship* as existing between God and some person or thing consecrated to Him. Yet such appears to be the real connotation of the root.

God Himself was regarded as "holy," One who from His nature, position, and attributes is to be set apart and revered as distinct from all others; Israel, too, was to separate itself from the world because God was thus separated (Leviticus 11:44, 19:2). In accordance with this teaching, therefore, the Lord was to be "sanctified," *i.e.*, regarded as occupying a unique position both morally and as concerns His essential nature (Leviticus 10:3; Psalm 111:9; Isaiah 6:3). But *kdsh* denotes more than position or relationship. It includes, as well, both the *act* and the *process* of setting apart for sacred use whereby that position or relationship is realized (Judges 17:3; 2 Samuel 8:11), and so approximates *nazar*, "to separate." In such cases it is to be translated as "dedicated" or "consecrated," indicating the transfer to the possession of God, to whom the person or thing dedicated now exclusively belongs.

Translators of the Septuagint (a Greek version of the Hebrew Old Testament, c. 150 B.C.) employed, almost invariably, the relatively little-used Greek adjective *hagios*, "holy" (literally, "not of the earth"), as a rendering of the Hebrew *kadosh*. They did not allow the Hebrew to be colored by the Greek meaning, but impressed *hagios* wholly into the service of *kadosh*. Philo and Josephus, influenced by Hellenistic currents and modes, did not maintain the same care in distinction; and in Rabbinic Judaism the negative side of the concept of holiness prevails, where "holy" and "chaste" come to be synonymous.

Hagios had been used but rarely in the Attic (classical) Greek. Its first certain attestation is in Herodotus, who brought it into close relationship to the sanctuary. Demosthenes also related it to the sanctuary, wherein the most beautiful and sacred things are not accessible to the public. In the Hellenistic period *hagios* found frequent expression as an epithet of the gods, but seems never to have been applied to men of the cultus. (*Hagnos*, in that respect, had taken its place.) It was used of customs connected with religion, especially the mysteries. *Hagios*, therefore, came into broad employment only in the Hellenistic period (as the Septuagint, Philo, and Josephus), and we must everywhere recognize the Semitic background of that employment.

In the New Testament, where *hagios* is used 235 times, God the Father is *hagios* (John 17:11; 1 Peter 1:15, 16), that truth being everywhere presumed but seldom stated; God the Son is *hagios* (John 6:69); and God the Spirit is *hagion* throughout. The Old Testament origin is obvious in Jerusalem's being called "the holy city" (Matthew 4:5); and thus we understand Paul's frequent application of the term both to the mother community in Jerusalem (Romans 15:25, 26) and to Gentile Christianity (Romans 1:7). Just as the Church militant stands under the concept of holiness, and so also the Church triumphant (Revelation 5:6, 7, 14:12), the life of the individual Christian, furthermore, should be "a living sacrifice, holy *(hagia)*, acceptable unto God" (Romans 12:1). The fundamental idea of *hagios*, then, like *kadosh*, is separation to the end of consecration and devotion to the service of the Deity.

Two Dimensions: Positional and Practical

The New Testament, moreover, presents the believer's personal separation and consecration to the purposes of God in terms of two aspects, positional and practical. God has the right to demand of us holiness of life; but because we cannot work out this holiness for ourselves, He freely effects it within us through the ministry of the Holy Spirit on the ground of the righteousness of Jesus Christ imputed to us. This is the burden of a rich array of Greek verbs in Hebrews 10, each of which connotes cleansing and perfecting in both objective and subjective relationships.[2]

Positional sanctification is experienced in the believer's new relationship to Christ subsequent to justification and regeneration. Such is Paul's burden in Romans 6:6-8, where he declares that "our old man is crucified with him, that the body of sin might be destroyed [better, *rendered inoperative*],

---

2 *Katharidzo, hagiadzo, teleioo, rantidzo,* and *louo,* all sacerdotal metaphors, in verses 2, 10, 14, and 22. See Charles Hodge, *Systematic Theology* (Grand Rapids, Michigan: Wm. B. Eerdmans Publishing Company, 1952), II, 510.

that henceforth we should not serve sin. For he that is dead is freed from sin. Now if we be dead with Christ, we believe that we shall also live with him."

The old relation to the law and sin, and the new relation to Christ and life, are further illustrated by the effect of death upon servitude (Romans 6:16-23) and marriage (Romans 7:1-6). Upon the strength of this regard the Apostle could announce to the Galatians that death to sin issues in life with Christ: "I am crucified with Christ: nevertheless I live; yet not I, but Christ liveth in me: and the life which I now live in the flesh I live by the faith of the Son of God, who loved me, and gave himself for me" (Galatians 2:20).

Practical sanctification is a pursuit of the devotional life. Were this not a valid distinction from the positional aspect, then Colossians 3:5 (Cf. 3:8), which urges us to "mortify [put to death] . . . [our] members which are upon earth . . ." would contradict rather than complement Paul's former citation in Romans 6:11: that believers "reckon" themselves to be "dead indeed unto sin, but alive unto God through Jesus Christ our Lord." By the same token, Paul could affirm that his Thessalonian readers were already sanctified, yet proceed to pray for their sanctification (2 Thessalonians 2:13; 1 Thessalonians 5: 23, 24); and so again he could disclaim to the Philippians any personal perfection, yet in the same breath assert that he *was* "perfect" (Philippians 3:12, 15).

If the practical aspect of sanctification also, as our Declaration of Faith affirms,[3] is subsequent to the new birth, how then is it realized? It is precisely at

---

3 See page 92; cf. John 17:17; Hebrews 13:12.

this juncture that differences of interpretation regarding the teaching often have arisen. But we must constantly take care never to allow controversy to depreciate the beauty of the doctrine of sanctification or to discredit its place of urgency in the ministry of the Church.

The *prerequisites* to practical sanctification, as we have noted to this point, are justification, the acquittal of guilt for acts of sin committed, constituting the legal ground for God's further dealing with the believer, and regeneration, the communication of divine life to the soul, being the imparting of a new nature. The *purposes* of practical sanctification are the establishment of a relationship to deity (separation) and the realization of a quality of life (cleansing). The *pursuit* of practical sanctification, in response to the former inquiry, is commended along these several lines:

(1) Neither justification nor regeneration ministers to the nature of sin. This lack is attested by the Scriptures, by the universal experience of Christians, and by the undeniable evidence of history. The Bible is replete with reports of the inward conflicts of the most eminent of God's servants, with their backslidings, their falls, their repentings, and their jeremiads or lamentings over continued "missings of the mark." It also fully describes the nature of the conflict between good and evil in the heart of the renewed, distinguishes and designates the contending principles, and sets forth repeatedly and in detail the necessities, difficulties, and perils of the struggle, as well as the method of properly sustaining it.

The principle of new life, then, as the ordinary

experience of God's people attests, may be very feeble, having much in the soul uncongenial with its nature, and the conflict between the old life and the new life may be protracted and painful. (See Romans 7:7-24.) The Apostle exclaimed:

> For I delight in the law of God after the inward man: But I see another law in my members, warring against the law of my mind, and bringing me into captivity to the law of sin which is in my members. O wretched man that I am! who shall deliver me from the body of this death? (Romans 7:22-24)

(2) In ministering to the nature of sin, the Holy Spirit continues His work begun in regeneration. Practical sanctification, then, is distinguished from regeneration as growth is distinguished from birth, or as the strengthening of a holy disposition from the original impartation of it. This appears to be the message in Philippians 1:6: "Being confident of this very thing, that he which hath begun a good work in you will perform it until the day of Jesus Christ."

(3) This particular experience wrought by the Holy Spirit must be sought earnestly by the believer. That which has commenced in crisis continues only by careful cultivation of the devotional life. Indeed, Berkhof has n o t e d that "it [sanctification] should never be represented as a merely natural process in the spiritual development of man, nor brought down to the level of a mere human achievement, as is done in a great deal of modern liberal theology."[4]

---

4 L. Berkhof, *Systematic Theology* (Grand Rapids, Michigan: Wm. B. Eerdmans Publishing Company, 1941), p. 533.

It is clear that Paul found resolution of his own spiritual vexation only in the release effected by the Holy Spirit:

> There is therefore now no condemnation to them which are in Christ Jesus, who walk not after the flesh, but after the Spirit. For the law of the Spirit of life in Christ Jesus hath made me free from the law of sin and death. (Romans 8:1, 2)

(4) To speak of the Holy Spirit's work in terms of continuance is in no way to suggest that that work is imperfect, as if only a part of the "new man" that originates in regeneration were affected.

> It is the whole, but yet undeveloped new man, that must grow into full stature. A new-born child is, barring exceptions, perfect in parts, but not yet in degree of development for which it is intended. Just so the new man is perfect in parts, but remains in the present life imperfect in the degree of spiritual development.[5]

This perspective renders more intelligible the Pauline admonition in Colossians 3:8-12 to "put off" and to "put on" (practically) what he had already "put off" and "put on" (positionally). (Cf. Romans 8:13; 2 Corinthians 7:1; Ephesians 4:11-15.) And it likewise assigns more substance to the Petrine injunction to "grow in grace, and in the knowledge of our Lord and Saviour Jesus Christ" (2 Peter 3:18).

(5) The practical dimension of sanctification, then, may be defined as "the work of God's free grace, whereby we are renewed in the whole man after the image of God, and are enabled more and

---

5 *Ibid.,* p. 537.

more to die unto sin, and live unto righteousness."[6]
The concept includes, furthermore, the following
rationale in terms of causality:

(a) The *formal* cause is the love of God (1
John 4:10);

(b) The *meritorious* cause is the blood of Jesus Christ (1 John 1:7);

(c) The *efficient* cause is the Holy Spirit
(Titus 3:5; 1 Peter 1:2);

(d) The *instrumental* cause is truth (*i.e.,* the
Word of God, John 17:17); and,

(e) The *conditional* cause is faith (Acts 15:
9, 26:18).

The pursuit of holiness is made mandatory in
Hebrews 12:14: "Follow peace with all men, and
holiness, without which no man shall see the Lord."
Hagiasmos, "holiness," is translated "sanctification"
in the American Standard Version. The word occurs in the New Testament only in the epistles, and
preponderently in the field of Gentile Christianity.
This noun, with its action terminus *-mos,* may be
rendered better still as "sanctifying." It is distinguished from *hagios* and *hagiadzo* by stress upon
the moral element.

Always presupposing that holiness obtained by
justification and regeneration, *hagiasmos* denotes the
work whereby one becomes separated unto God in
his entire life and conduct. In other words, he who
is already *hagios* by faith is ever to continue in

---

6 Westminster Shorter Catechism, Article 35.

pursuit of *hagiasmos* in daily experience.[7] F. F. Bruce reminds us that " 'the sanctification without which no man shall see the Lord' is, as the words themselves make plain, no optional extra in the Christian life but something which belongs to its essence."[8]

Does a Christian Ever Sin?

The very nature of the divine admonition in Hebrews 12:14 naturally provokes a point of inquiry: Does a Christian ever sin? Is this a valid prospect? If so, how does it relate to the pursuit of holiness?

Several observations seem to be appropriate at the outset. First, this basic inquiry too often has been evaded at the expense of truth and genuine spiritual blessing. Second, such questioning has been thought divisive, aligning respondents into two contrary camps: the so-called conservatives, who contend for a sinless perfection, and the so-called liberals, who discern a license to sin. Third, while the Christian must always be very careful to identify sin as just that very thing, he must exercise the same care to distinguish between what is really sin and what is merely personal opinion, preference, or taste, or what is culturally imposed. The gospel of Jesus Christ never separates true believers; rather, it accentuates their common ground (see Ephesians

---

7 R. C. H. Lenski, *The Interpretation of the Epistle to the Hebrews* (Columbus: The Wartburg Press, 1956), p. 443. Cf. Robert W. Funk, *A Greek Grammar of the New Testament and Other Early Christian Literature* (Chicago: University of Chicago Press, 1961), pp. 58-9.

8 F. F. Bruce, *The Epistle to the Hebrews* (in *The New International Commentary on the New Testament;* Grand Rapids, Michigan: Wm. B. Eerdmans Publishing Company, 1964), p. 364.

4:4-6), while allowing a law of Christian liberty (Romans 14).

A proper resolution to the problem begins with the recollection that Holy Scripture is sufficiently explicit in condemnation of sinful living. Such pursuits constitute the sinner as contrary to the will of God and devoid of his grace in Christ. But when he becomes reconciled to the Father, his interests lie in terms of a higher plane and a nobler calling (2 Corinthians 5:17). That he should live thereafter in sin so grace might abound is both inconsistent with his newly acquired status and offensive to his renewed spiritual sensibilities (Romans 6:1).

No experience of grace, however, transfers the Christian to some plane in advance of humanity, where he is rendered immune to temptation and positioned beyond the possibility of sinning. While the *power* of sin has been broken for the recipient of grace, the *presence* of sin and the *possibility* of sinning remain very real. This tension must necessarily be the experience of every believer.

It is precisely to this tension that John addresses his general appeal. Having insisted that his "little children" sin not, he hastens to announce a gracious provision for any who should do so. "If any man sin," he declares, "we have an advocate with the Father, Jesus Christ the righteous: And he is the propitiation for our sins: and not for our's only, but also for the sins of the whole world" (1 John 2:1, 2). Herein lies the victory over personal sin. Jesus Christ, sustaining His own through a continuum of cleansing by His own blood, acts as advocate—or lawyer—on our behalf before the throne of grace.

(The word "advocate" here in the Greek *parakletos,* used also of the Holy Spirit in John 14:16, 16:7.)

Sincere repentance for sins committed is the condition upon which this remedial provision is appropriated. John, therefore, while he acknowledges the possibility of a Christian's sinning (1 John 2:1), nowhere allows for "sinning Christians" (1 John 5:18). According to his own word in extended context, he that *practices* sin is of the devil. (This is the intention of the Greek tense employed in 1 John 3:8, 9). John's rationale of repentance in its fullest dimension should encourage every Christian in his pursuit of "the measure of the stature of the fulness of Christ" (Ephesians 4:13).

And did not our Lord Himself charge us to pray, "Forgive us our debts [*i.e.,* sins], as we forgive our debtors [*i.e.,* those who sin against us]"? (Matthew 6:12). When prompted by the Holy Spirit, repentance effects forgiveness and restores the believer's redemptive relationship with God. Having been tempted in all points as we are (Hebrews 4:15), Jesus Christ our High Priest pleads intelligently and empathetically for every repentant and contrite heart.

That a Christian *can* willfully forfeit eternal life and ultimately be lost is a possibility which the Bible allows (John 15:1-7; Galatians 5:4). But while the Scriptures nowhere admit an "eternal security," to forfeit eternal life may be more difficult than is frequently alleged, considering the marvelous spiritual resources in accruement to the believer, *e.g.,* the righteousness of Christ imputed, the indwelling of the Holy Spirit, and numerous blessings in pursuit of practical sanctification. When God saves and sanctifies us for the sake of His Son, He does not take lightly that copious bestowal of grace. We become His children, and He our Father; and that relationship so sustained is no tenuous commitment. (See John 10:28; Romans 8:35-39; Ephesians 1:13, 4:30.)

Lessons in Holiness

At least seven lessons of practical import may be itemized in summary of all the foregoing considerations:

(1) Holiness derives from the personal God, who is Himself holy;

(2) Holiness is a quality supernaturally conferred, not naturally possessed, from the underived holiness which belongs to God alone;

(3) Holiness is a quality assigned to those persons and things brought into relationship with God, not something simulated by cult, ritual, observance, ceremonial, or tradition;

(4) Holiness is of an objective nature, with the blood and righteousness of Jesus Christ as its ground;

(5) Holiness is of a subjective nature, tantamount to sanctification, with the pursuit of renewal in the Holy Spirit as its rationale and end;

(6) Holiness is an activity as well as a status, extrinsic as well as intrinsic, finding expression in one's relationships to his fellowmen;

(7) Holiness, in these various nuances of the concept, constitutes the essence, never the option, of the Christian life.

GLORIFICATION

Since God must make man holy, if ever he is to be holy, man must yield himself to God that He may accomplish this work in him. Entire conformity to Christ, the culmination of that sanctification essential to "seeing the Lord" (Hebrews 12:14), will be realized as a final ministry of the Holy Spirit in his behalf. Whereas justification remits the *penalty* of sin, and sanctification inhibits the *power* of sin, glorification transfers the believer beyond the *presence* of sin. Thus to be saved eternally and incontrovertibly is the blessed hope of the Christian.

Salvation from the presence of sin occurs either at the second coming of the Lord (1 Thessalonians 3:13; Hebrews 9:28; Jude 23) or at death (Hebrews 12:23). At the first resurrection, all those in Christ—both dead and living—will be raptured together to meet the Lord (1 Thessalonians 4:13-18); "in a moment, in the twinkling of an eye," Paul promises, ". . . we shall be changed (1 Corinthians 15:52).

This wonderful prospect of complete maturation is predicated upon our Lord's own triumph over death, hell, and the grave; and during the interim it impels to all circumspection in conduct. John writes: "Beloved, now are we the sons of God, and it doth not yet appear what we shall be: but we know that, when he shall appear, we shall be like him; for we shall see him as he is. And every man that hath this hope in him purifieth himself, even as he is pure" (1 John 3:2, 3).

The Bible discusses more the prospect of glorification than the pattern. As John has told us, "we shall be like Him"; but what is the nature of Jesus' glorified body it does not tell us certainly. (See Luke 24:39-43; John 20:19, 20, 21:9, 10, 13; 1 Corinthians 13:12, 15:50.) But on that grand day, "this corruptible must put on incorruption, and this mortal must put on immortality" (1 Corinthians 15:53); on that grand day He "shall change our vile body, that it may be fashioned like unto his glorious body, according to the working whereby he is able even to subdue all things unto himself" (Philippians 3:21).

". . . And . . . them he also glorified" (Romans 8:30). The Apostle speaks here of that event foreknown by God from eternity, and which all His ministries in application by the Holy Spirit have anticipated. Glorification completes the *ordo salutis*, constituting the ultimate triumph of grace.

Soli Deo Gloria!

SUMMARY QUESTIONS

1. Define: sanctification, paraclete, security, holiness, glorification.

2. Distinguish between *positional* and *practical* aspects of sanctification.

3. Along what lines does the Bible draw a rationale for the pursuit of practical sanctification?

4. What is the Christian's recourse if he sins?

5. What practical lessons do the Scriptures teach regarding holiness?

8 The Mission
of the Church

Application of redemption embraces more than those ministries of the Holy Spirit delineated in an order of salvation. The benefits of grace obligate their recipients to the discharge of certain responsibilities commensurate with new perspective and motivation. Redemption creates a community, constrains Christians to proclaim its message, and challenges them to Christian involvement in a modern world.

THE FELLOWSHIP OF THE REDEEMED

A study of the *ordo salutis* issues in the indelible impression that all Christians have been brought into fellowship through the blood and righteousness of Jesus Christ procuring eternal salvation. Collectively, they constitute the Church, the Body of Jesus Christ. The word "church," *ecclesia,* derived from *ek* and *kaleo,* refers to the "called out ones."[1]

---

1 *Ecclesia* was from the first a secular expression, denoting a popular assembly called together by the herald. "This teaches us something concerning the biblical and Christian usage, namely, that God in Christ calls men out of the world." Gerhard Kittel (ed.), *Theological Dictionary of the New Testament,* trans. Geoffrey W. Bromiley (Grand Rapids, Michigan: Wm. B. Eerdmans Publishing Company, 1964-), III, 513.

By the grace of God in Jesus Christ, those now His own have been summoned from the world to pursuit of a new vocation.

John Calvin defined the Church, the company of the redeemed, as "the society of all the saints, a society which, spread over the whole world, and existing in all ages, yet bound together by the one doctrine and the one Spirit of Christ, cultivates and observes unity of faith and brotherly concord."[2] The Great Genevan was but applying the Pauline concept of the Church urged by the Apostle upon a factious body in his own time (see 1 Corinthians 12:12-27). It follows from this designation, then, that all narrow proscription must necessarily yield to the truth of common ground.

Word and sacrament convince the sincere believer of this enlarged conception of *ecclesia*. Word and sacrament continue to constrain him toward labor in that wider context where vital integration of privilege and mission becomes better discerned. Fully respecting his responsibility to his own communion, every Christian in the process of genuine spiritual maturation discovers the joyous commonality of that larger and truly universal whole, designed for the ultimate honor and praise of Jesus Christ.

Contemporary Pentecostalism, in particular, needs to perceive this blessed tie that binds. It must disclaim any divisive "third force" designation that some would assign, and come rather to discern unmistakably its identification with historic Protestantism. To perpetuate its worthwhile distinctives

2 John Calvin, "Reply to Sadoleto," in *A Reformation Debate,* ed. John C. Olin (New York: Harper and Row, 1966), p. 62.

without pretense of exclusivism is the present challenge, and by so doing to cultivate an appreciation for the broader evangelical fellowship.

THE MINISTRY OF RECONCILIATION

Christianity is sharing. Having been redeemed by the blood of Jesus Christ, members of His Church eagerly communicate the gospel through a variety of means. Paul gives us the charge:

> Therefore if any man be in Christ, he is a new creature: old things are passed away; behold, all things are become new. And all things are of God, who hath reconciled us to himself by Jesus Christ, and *hath given to us the ministry of reconciliation;* to wit, that God was in Christ, reconciling the world unto himself, not imputing their trespasses unto them; and *hath committed unto us the word of reconciliation.* Now then we are ambassadors *for Christ,* as though God *did beseech you by us:* we pray you *in Christ's stead,* be ye reconciled to God. For he hath made him to be sin for us, who knew no sin; that we might be made the righteousness of God in him. (2 Corinthians 5:17-21)

It is clear from these verses that the Christian is an "ambassador" (*presbuteros*) of God dispatched with the message of "reconciliation" (*katallage*). A *presbuteros,* in both civil and religious contexts, was:

(1) One mature, having the advantage of experience;

(2) One responsible, not for his own word, but for the word of another whom he served;

(3) One charged to bring hostiles into the kingdom;

(4) One never ashamed to implore, if necessary, because of the nobility of his calling; and,

(5) One representing another in his name and authority.

A thoroughly responsible emissary, the *presbuteros* was commissioned to bear an urgent message. *Katallage* refers to:

(1) A change or exchange of any kind, such as of garment, shape, money, or status;

(2) A bringing together of people f o r m e r l y estranged;

(3) A restoration of fellowship between man and God; and,

(4) An attraction of man to God, never of God to man.[3]

To discharge this responsibility of communication, Christians must go out of the church and into the world, *i.e.*, they must carry their devotion to Christ beyond four walls, pulpit, altar, and pew, and into a secularized, polarized, technocentric society that needs the word of His grace so desperately. The tragic mistake of too many Christians is that they confuse service with worship. Worship precedes, service follows; worship retires, service performs; worship edifies, service expends. Neither is a substitute for the other; each is complementary to the other. These two aspects—internal and external—of pure and undefiled religion (see James

---

3 See William Barclay, *More New Testament Words* (New York: Harper and Brothers, 1958), pp. 102-6.

1:27) must always be properly related. How often we worship, but how seldom we truly serve!

Dietrich Bonhoeffer asserts that costly grace is turned into cheap grace without dynamic discipleship. A "holy-worldliness," *i.e.*, practicing the holiness of Jesus Christ in a society hostile to holiness, is the most effective communication to this generation. But

> the Church confesses that she has not proclaimed often and clearly enough her message of the one God who has revealed Himself for all times in Jesus Christ and who suffers no other gods beside Himself. She confesses her timidity, her evasiveness, her dangerous concessions. . . . By her own silence she has rendered herself guilty of the decline in responsible action, in bravery in the defence of a cause, and in willingness to suffer for what is known to be right.[4]

The Church must learn to say "no" to sin but "yes" to the sinner; it must develop an aggressive "this-sidedness"; it must be *in* the world. [5] (Cf. John 17:9, 11, 15-17.)

Jesus addressed this very matter so long ago when He promised that "ye shall receive power, after that the Holy Ghost is come upon you: and ye shall be witnesses unto me . . ." (Acts 1:8). Power is the essence of the baptism with the Holy Spirit. Just as power for service was the distinctive of the early Church, so now it must be evident in any com-

---

4 Dietrich Bonhoeffer, *Ethics*, ed. Eberhard Bethge, trans. Neville Horton Smith (New York: The Macmillan Company, 1965), pp. 113, 115.
5 Dietrich Bonhoeffer, *The Cost of Discipleship*, trans. Reginald H. Fuller (New York: The Macmillan Company, 1959), *passim.* Cf. H. Richard Niebuhr, *Christ and Culture* (New York: Harper & Row, 1956), *passim.*

munity purporting to bear His name and to further the cause of His kingdom.

THE CONTINUING QUEST FOR RELEVANCE

Christianity is not so much a series of experiences as it is a way of life. Our commitment is neither to tradition nor to program, but to a Person and to an emulation of His graces. Although the pursuit of certain blessings is enjoined in the Scripture, these in themselves do not constitute the essence of Christian existence and endeavor. Every seeker-after-God may, assuredly, reflect upon precious moments in His presence; but unless these periodic encounters with deity motivate the believer to fruitful life and service, where is the profit for the purposes of Christ in the world?

The Church is encumbered today by a disposition that promotes spiritual experience in isolation from daily interaction. While the case for personal religion is sound scripturally, yet another dimension to Christian experience and expression is commended from that elemental base. That devotion to God should be divorced from service in the world is untenable, for the constancy and consistency proceeding from genuine love for both God and man are maximal evidences of the transformed life.

As the Body of Christ with His mission to perform, the Church is responsible for utilizing every resource at its disposal. These resources are human as well as divine. The Church will become relevant in corresponding proportion to its perceptive employment of those dedicated minds and means that God has placed within its charge. This we must understand as nothing less than positive commitment to education, to democratic involvement of laity, and to responsible social action. Each is wholly supportive of the charge to witness in the world.

Nothing is more relevant than the message of redemption, nor anything so contemporary as the urgency of salvation. The syntax of our time is exceedingly complicated. The Church must, therefore, learn the language of the gospel, the language of the world, and the art of translation.

SUMMARY QUESTIONS

1. Define: church, fellowship, reconciliation, "holy-worldliness," relevance.

2. Describe an "ambassador" of Jesus Christ.

3. Christianity is not so much a series of experiences as it is a way of life. Explain.

4. How should the believer relate to his own communion? to the Church at large?

5. Relate education, involvement of laity, and social action to the evangelistic charge of the Church.

BIBLIOGRAPHY

Arndt, William F. and F. Wilbur Gingrich, *A Greek-English Lexicon of the New Testament and Other Early Christian Literature.* Chicago: University of Chicago Press, 1959.

Augustine, Aurelius. *De Civitate Dei.* In *A Select Library of the Nicene and Post-Nicene Fathers of the Christian Church,* ed. Philip Schaff. First series; fourteen volumes. Grand Rapids, Michigan: Wm. B. Eerdmans Publishing Company, 1956.

_____. *De Genesi ad Litteram.* In *A Select Library of the Nicene and Post-Nicene Fathers of the Christian Church,* ed. Philip Schaff. First series; fourteen volumes. Grand Rapids, Michigan: Wm. B. Eerdmans Publishing Company, 1956.

_____. *Quaestionum in Heptateuchum.* In *A Select Library of the Nicene and Post-Nicene Fathers of the Christian Church,* ed. Philip Schaff. First series, fourteen volumes. Grand Rapids, Michigan: Wm. B. Eerdmans Publishing Company, 1956.

Barclay, William. *More New Testament Words.* New York: Harper & Brothers, 1958.

Barth, Karl. *Dogmatics in Outline.* New York: Harper & Brothers, 1959.

Berkhof, L. *Systematic Theology.* Grand Rapids, Michigan: Wm. B. Eerdmans Publishing Company, 1941.

Black, Hubert P. "The Problem of Evil," *Christianity Today,* XV (April 23, 1971), 12.

Bonhoeffer, Dietrich. *The Cost of Discipleship.* Trans. Reginald H. Fuller. New York: The Macmillan Company, 1959.

_____. *Ethics.* Ed. Eberhard Bethge. Trans. Neville Horton Smith. New York: The Macmillan Company, 1965.

Bowdle, Donald N. (ed.). *Ellicott's Bible Commentary.* Grand Rapids, Michigan: Zondervan Publishing House, 1971.

Brown, Francis, S. R. Driver, and Charles A. Briggs, *A Hebrew and English Lexicon of the Old Testament.* Oxford: Oxford University Press, 1907.

Bruce, F. F. *The Book of Acts*. In *The New International Commentary on the New Testament*. Grand Rapids, Michigan: Wm. B. Eerdmans Publishing Company, 1956.

——————. *The Epistle to the Hebrews*. In *The New International Commentary on the New Testament*. Grand Rapids, Michigan: Wm. B. Eerdmans Publishing Company, 1964.

Calvin, John. *Institutes of the Christian Religion*. Trans. Henry Beveridge. Three volumes. Grand Rapids, Michigan: Wm. B. Eerdmans Publishing Company, 1962.

——————. "Reply to Sadoleto." In *A Reformation Debate*, ed. John C. Olin. New York: Harper & Row, 1966.

Carnell, Edward John. *An Introduction to Christian Apologetics; A Philosophic Defense of the Trinitarian-Theistic Faith*. Grand Rapids, Michigan: Wm. B. Eerdmans Publishing Company, 1948.

Church of God Declaration of Faith, Articles 6, 7.

Conn, Charles W. *Why Men Go Back; Studies in Defection and Devotion*. Cleveland, Tennessee: Pathway Press, 1966.

Engel, David E. "Educating the Layman Theologically," *Theology Today*, XXX (July, 1964), 196-205.

Fairbairn, Patrick. *The Revelation of Law in Scripture*. Grand Rapids, Michigan: Zondervan Publishing House, 1957.

Fisher, George P. *The Grounds of Theistic and Christian Belief*. New York: Charles Scribner's Sons, 1897.

Funk, Robert W. *A Grammar of the Greek New Testament and Other Early Christian Literature*. Chicago: University of Chicago Press, 1961.

Girdlestone, Robert B. *Synonyms of the Old Testament*. Grand Rapids, Michigan: Wm. B. Eerdmans Publishing Company, 1897.

Hodge, Charles. *An Exposition of the Second Epistle to the Corinthians*. Grand Rapids, Michigan: Wm. B. Eerdmans Publishing Company, n.d.

——————. *Systematic Theology*. Three volumes. Grand Rapids, Michigan: Wm. B. Eerdmans Publishing Company, 1952.

Kittel, Gerhard (ed.). *Theological Dictionary of the New Testament.* Seven volumes. Trans. Geoffrey W. Bromiley. Grand Rapids, Michigan: Wm. B. Eerdmans Publishing Company, 1964-.

Lenski, R. C. H. *The Interpretation of the Epistle to the Hebrews.* Columbus: The Wartburg Press, 1956.

Leupold, H. C. *Exposition of Genesis.* Two volumes. Grand Rapids, Michigan: Baker Book House, 1942.

Liddell, Henry George and Robert Scott. *A Greek-English Lexicon.* Ninth edition. Oxford: Oxford University Press, 1940.

Lightfoot, J. B. *The Epistle of St. Paul to the Galatians.* Second edition. Grand Rapids, Michigan: Zondervan Publishing House, 1957.

Nicoll, W. Robertson (ed.). *The Expositor's Greek Testament.* Five volumes. Grand Rapids, Michigan: Wm. B. Eerdmans Publishing Company, 1956.

Niebuhr, H. Richard. *Christ and Culture.* New York: Harper & Row, 1956.

Orr, James, *et. al.* (eds.). *The International Standard Bible Encyclopedia.* Five volumes. Grand Rapids, Michigan: Wm. B. Eerdmans Publishing Company, 1939.

Outler, Albert C. *Who Trusts in God: Musings on the Meaning of Providence.* New York: Oxford University Press, 1968.

Payne, J. Barton. *The Theology of the Older Testament.* Grand Rapids, Michigan: Zondervan Publishing House, 1962.

Ramm, Bernard. *The Christian View of Science and Scripture.* Grand Rapids, Michigan: Wm. B. Eerdmans Publishing Company, 1954.

Richardson, Alan (ed.). *A Theological Wordbook of the Bible.* New York: The Macmillan Company, 1950.

Robertson, A. T. *A Grammar of the Greek New Testament in the Light of Historical Research.* Nashville: Broadman Press, 1934.

Sanday, William and Arthur C. Headlam. *The Epistle to the Romans*. Eleventh edition. In *The International Critical Commentary*, ed. Charles A. Briggs, S. R. Driver, and Alfred Plummer. New York: Charles Scribner's Sons, 1906.

Sauer, Erich. *The Dawn of World Redemption; A Survey of Historical Revelation in the Old Testament*. Trans. G. H. Lang. Grand Rapids, Michigan: Wm. B. Eerdmans Publishing Company, 1955.

_____. *The Triumph of the Crucified; A Survey of Historical Revelation in the New Testament*. Trans. G. H. Lang. Grand Rapids, Michigan: Wm. B. Eerdmans Publishing Company, 1955.

Schaeffer, Francis A. *The God Who is There; Speaking Historic Christianity into the Twentieth Century*. Downers Grove, Illinois: Inter-Varsity Press, 1968.

Shedd, Wm. G. T. *Dogmatic Theology*. Three volumes. New York: Charles Scribner's Sons, 1889.

Slay, James L. *This We Believe*. Cleveland, Tennessee: Pathway Press, 1963.

Strong, Augustus Hopkins. *Systematic Theology*. Philadelphia: The Judson Press, 1907.

Thayer, Joseph Henry. *A Greek-English Lexicon of the New Testament*. Fourth edition. Edinburgh: T & T Clark, 1901.

Thiessen, Henry C. *Introductory Lectures in Systematic Theology*. Grand Rapids, Michigan: Wm. B. Eerdmans Publishing Company, 1949.

Trench, Richard C. *Synonyms of the New Testament*. Grand Rapids, Michigan: Wm. B. Eerdmans Publishing Company, 1958.

Triplett, Bennie S. *A Contemporary Study of the Holy Spirit*. Cleveland, Tennessee: Pathway Press, 1970.

Warfield, Benjamin Breckinridge. *Biblical and Theological Studies*. Ed. Samuel G. Craig. Philadelphia: The Presbyterian and Reformed Publishing Company, 1952.

_____. *Calvin and Augustine*. Ed. Samuel G. Craig.

Philadelphia: The Presbyterian and Reformed Publishing Company, 1956.

_____. *The Inspiration and Authority of the Bible.* Ed. Samuel G. Craig. Philadelphia: The Presbyterian and Reformed Publishing Company, 1948.

Westcott, Brooke Foss. *Epistle to the Ephesians.* London: Macmillan and Company, Limited, 1906.

Westminster Shorter Catechism, Articles 18, 19, 33, 35.

Wiley, H. Orton. *Christian Theology.* Three volumes. Kansas City: Beacon Hill Press, 1952.

Wyckoff, D. Campbell. "The Gospel Empowering the Teaching Church," *The Princeton Seminary Bulletin,* LV (January, 1962), 48-60.

INSTRUCTIONS FOR PREPARING A
WRITTEN REVIEW

1. A certificate of credit will be awarded when the student satisfies the requirements listed on page 7.

2. The student, at a time designated by the instructor, should prepare the written review following the guidelines listed below. The student should use blank sheets of paper and make his own outline for the review. The complete written review should be presented to the instructor for processing.

3. In the case of home study, the student should present his answers to the pastor or someone whom he may designate.

REDEMPTION ACCOMPLISHED AND APPLIED

by Donald N. Bowdle, Ph.D., Th.D.

CTC 304 — Written Review

1. List two differences between naturalism and supernaturalism.
2. Describe how man is made in the image of God.
3. Give a brief definition of the following words: evil, providence, depravity, imputation.
4. Explain why Christian theism is the only answer to the problem of evil.
5. Describe how the fall of Adam affected the human race.
6. List the three reasons for the progress of the revelation of redemption.
7. Name two types of Christ that appear in the Old Testament.
8. List the five facets of the election of God as described by Paul.
9. Explain the expression "eternal plan of God."
10. Explain why the baptism with the Holy Spirit is not a part of salvation.
11. Explain the basic difference between repentance and conversion.

12. List the four things the Scriptures teach as to the method of justification.

13. List three important aspects of repentance.

14. Define the following words: regeneration, temperance, union, adoption, conformity.

15. Explain the difference between the indwelling and the infilling of the Holy Spirit.

16. List the nine fruit of the Spirit as recorded in Galatians 5:22, 23.

17. Write a brief definition of the following five words: sanctification, paraclete, security, holiness, glorification.

18. Distinguish between the positional and practical aspects of sanctification.

19. Explain the Christian's recourse if he sins.

20. List the seven lessons of practical import of holiness as itemized by the author.

21. Give a brief definition of the following words: church, reconciliation, "holy-worldliness," relevance.

22. Explain what it means to be an "ambassador" of Jesus Christ.

23. Explain why Christianity is not so much a series of experiences as it is a way of life.

24. Explain why education, involvement of laity, and social action are involved in the evangelistic charge of the church.

25. Write a brief paragraph on the subject: "What This Training Course Has Meant to Me."